D1407586

C Made Easy

Herbert Schildt

Osborne **McGraw-Hill**
Berkeley, California

Published by
Osborne **McGraw-Hill**
2600 Tenth Street
Berkeley, California 94710
U.S.A.

For information on translations and book distributors outside of the U.S.A.,
please write to Osborne **McGraw-Hill** at the above address.

C MADE EASY

1234567890 DODO 898765

ISBN 0-07-881178-3

Jon Erickson, Acquisitions Editor
Lorraine Aochi, Technical Editor
Raymond Lauzzana, Technical Reviewer
Ted Gartner, Copy Editor
Judy Wohlfrom, Text Design
Deborah Wilson, Composition
Yashi Okita, Cover Design

DEDICATION

To my lovely wife Sheryl, without whose help this book would not have been possible.

C Made Easy

C O N T E N T S

INTRODUCTION

The purpose of this book is to teach you the C programming language. Because programming is learned best by doing, it is strongly recommended that you have access to a C compiler. There are several available for most microcomputers, including excellent ones for the IBM PC and compatibles. The examples presented in the book will compile correctly and without errors on virtually any C compiler. However, minor variances can occur among different compilers, so it is best to check your user manual first.

This book assumes that you have some knowledge of programming. You should understand the general concepts of variables, assignment statements, and loops. Don't worry, your programming experience need not be extensive.

Because BASIC is generally included with the computer when you purchase it, you are probably acquainted with it. BASIC has become a common language for program examples because it is so widely known. Expecially in the earlier chapters of this book, BASIC and C examples will be used side by side to help you better understand aspects of the C language. Sometimes, seeing a statement written in a language that you are learning is worth more than pages of explanation. However, knowledge of BASIC is not required. Even if you don't know BASIC, this book will still be excellent for learning the C programming language.

If you have not yet purchased a compiler, it is strongly recommended that you buy one that is *UNIX-compatible*, because the function library that comes with it will be similar to the one described in this book.

In the early examples, data will be input to programs using either the **getchar( )** function, which is found with most compilers, or the **getnum( )** function, which is developed in the text as an easy way to input decimal numbers.

The examples in this book were compiled and run using the Aztec C compiler for the IBM PC. The examples will also compile and run using the SuperSoft C compiler, with the exception that the floating-point examples may need to be changed slighty to accommodate differences in the SuperSoft implementation. In general, any version 7, UNIX-compatible compiler will compile and run the programs in this book.

Introducing C

C H A P T E R   1

C is often called a middle-level computer language. *Middle-level* does not have a negative meaning: it does not mean that C is less powerful, harder to use, or less developed than a high-level language such as BASIC or Pascal; nor does it mean that C is similar to a low-level language, such as assembly language (often called *assembler*), which is simply a symbolic representation of the actual machine code a computer can read. C is a middle-level language because it combines elements of a high-level language with the functionalism of assembler. Table 1-1 shows the levels of various computer languages, including C.

A middle-level language gives programmers a minimal set of control and data-manipulation statements that they can use to define high-level constructs. In contrast, a high-level language is designed to try to give programmers everything they could possibly want already built into the language. A low-level language forces programmers to define all program functions directly because nothing is built-in. One approach is not inherently better than the other; each has its specific application. Middle-level languages are sometimes thought of as building-block languages because the

Table 1-1. Levels of Computer Languages

High Level	Middle Level	Low Level
Ada	C	Assembler
BASIC	FORTH	
COBOL		
FORTRAN		
Pascal		

programmer first creates the routines to perform all the program's necessary functions and then puts them together.

C allows—indeed needs—the programmer to define routines to perform high-level commands. These routines are called *functions* and are very important in the C language. You can easily tailor a library of C functions to perform tasks that are carried out by your program. In this sense, you can personalize C to fit your needs.

As a middle-level language C manipulates the bits, bytes, and addresses the computer functions with. Unlike BASIC, a high-level language that can operate directly on strings of characters to perform a multitude of string functions, C can operate directly on characters. In BASIC, there are built-in statements to read and write disk files. In C, these procedures are performed by functions that are not part of the C language proper, but are provided in the C standard library. These functions are special routines written in C that perform these operations. For example, the PRINT statement in BASIC has no direct parallel in C. However, there is a function called **printf ()** in your C compiler's standard function library that the manufacturer provided.

C does have its benefits. It has very few statements to remember—only 28 keywords. (The IBM PC version of BASIC has 159.) This means that C compilers can be written reasonably easily, so there is generally one available for your machine. Since C operates on the same data types as the computer, the code output from a C compiler is efficient and fast. C can be used in place of assembler for most tasks.

C code is very portable. *Portability* means software written for one type of computer can be adapted to another type. For example, if a program written for an Apple II+ can be easily moved to an IBM PC, that program is portable. Portability is important if you plan to use a new computer with a different processor. Most application programs will only need to be recompiled with a C compiler written for the new processor. This can save countless hours and dollars.

Uses of C

C was first used for system programming. *System programming* refers to a class of programs that either are part of or work closely with the operating system of the computer. System programs make the computer capable of performing useful work. These are examples of system programs that are often written in C:

- Operating systems
- Assemblers
- Print spoolers
- Modem programs
- Language interpreters

- Language compilers
- Text editors
- Network drivers
- Data bases
- Utilities

There are several reasons why C is used for system programming. System programs often must run very quickly. Programs compiled by C compilers can run almost as fast as those written in assembler. In the past, most system software had to be written in assembly language because none of the available computer languages could create programs that ran fast enough. Writing in assembly language is hard, tedious work. Since C code can be written more quickly than assembly code, using C reduces costs tremendously.

Another reason that C is frequently used for system programming is that it is a programmer's language. Professional programmers seem to be attracted to C because it lacks restrictions and easily manipulates bits, bytes, and addresses. The system programmer needs C's direct control of the I/O and memory management functions. C also allows a program to reflect the personality of the programmer.

Because programmers like to program in C, it has in recent years also been used as a general-purpose programming language. C is very readable. Once you are familiar with C, you can follow the precise flow and logic of a program and easily verify the general operation of subroutines. C program listings look clear; in contrast, a language like BASIC looks cluttered and confusing. Perhaps the best reason that C has become a general-purpose language is that it is simply fun to use.

C as
A Structured
Language

C is a structured language, as are Ada and Pascal. BASIC, COBOL, and FORTRAN are nonstructured languages. The most distinguishing feature of a structured language is that it uses blocks. A *block* is a set of statements that are logically connected. For example, imagine an IF statement that, if successful, will execute five discrete statements. If these statements can be grouped together and referenced easily, they form a block.

A structured language gives you a variety of programming possibilities. It supports the concept of subroutines with local variables. A *local variable* is simply a variable that is known only to the subroutine in which it is defined. A structured language also supports several loop constructs, such as the **while, do-while,** and **for** constructs. (The use of the **goto** is either prohibited or discouraged and is not the common form of program control in the same way it is in BASIC or FORTRAN.) A structured language allows separately compiled subroutines to be used without being in the program proper. This means that you can create a subroutine library of useful, tested functions that can be accessed by any program you write. A structured language allows you to indent statements and does not require a strict field concept as in FORTRAN.

Structured languages tend to be more modern, while the nonstructured are older. In fact, a characteristic of an old computer language is that it is not structured. Because of their clarity, structured languages are not only easier to program in but also much easier to maintain.

Although you may be able to think of nonstructured languages that still satisfy the requirements of a structured language (such as advanced BASICs), a structured language is based on the compartmentalization of function and data: that is, the reduction of each task to its own subroutine or block of code. As you learn the C programming language, the difference between a structured and nonstructured language will become quite clear.

Interpreters
Versus Compilers

The terms *interpreter* and *compiler* refer to how a program is executed. In theory any programming language can be either compiled or interpreted, but some languages are usually executed one way or the other. However, the way a program is executed is not defined by the language in which it is written. Interpreters and compilers are simply sophisticated programs that operate on your program source code. *Source code* is the program text that you write.

An interpreter reads the source code of your program one line at a time and performs the specific instructions contained in that line. A compiler reads the entire program and converts it into *object code*, which is a translation of the program source code into a form that can be directly executed by the computer. Object code is also referred to as *binary code* or *machine code*. Once the program is compiled, a line of source code is no longer meaningful to the execution of your program.

For example, BASIC is generally interpreted and C is almost always compiled. An interpreter must be present each time you run your program. In BASIC, you have to execute the BASIC interpreter first, load your program, and then type **RUN** each time you want to use the program. A compiler, on the other hand, converts your program into object code that can be directly executed by the computer. Because the compiler translates the program one time, all you need do in C is execute your program directly, generally by typing its name.

Compiled programs run much faster than interpreted ones. However, the compiling process itself does take more time. But this is easily offset by the time you save while using the program. The only time this is not true is if your program is very short—say, less than 50 lines—and does not use any loops.

In addition to the advantages of speed, compilers protect your source code from theft and unauthorized tampering. Compiled code bears no resemblance to source code, and this is the reason compilers are used almost exclusively by commercial software houses.

Two terms you will see often in this book and in your C compiler manual are *compile time* and *run time*. Compile time refers to the events that occur during the compilation process. Run time refers to the events that occur while the program is actually executing. Unfortunately, you will often see them used in connection with the word *error*, as in *compile-time errors* and *run-time errors*.

General Overview of C

CHAPTER 2

Before learning any specific information about C, you should see what a C program looks like compared to its BASIC equivalent. This chapter will go over C fundamentals; the later chapters will thoroughly explain all aspects of the C programming language.

Figure 2-1 gives the first program beginners usually write in C or BASIC. The program simply prints the word **HELLO** on the computer's screen followed by a carriage return/line feed combination.

Functions in C

The C language is based on the concept of building blocks. The building blocks are called *functions*. A C program is a collection of one or more functions. To write a program, you first create functions and then put them together.

```
main()
{                              10 PRINT "HELLO"
       printf("HELLO\n");      20 END
}
```

Figure 2-1. C version and BASIC version of a program that prints **HELLO**

A function is a subroutine that contains one or more C statements and performs one or more tasks. In well-written C code, each function performs only one task. Each function has a name and a list of arguments that the function will receive. In general, you can give a function whatever name you please, with the exception of **main**, which is reserved for the function that begins program execution.

When denoting functions, this book uses a convention that has become standard when writing about C: a function will have parentheses after the function name. For example, if a function's name is **max**, it would be written as **max()**. This notation will help distinguish variable names from function names.

In the HELLO program of Figure 2-1 both **main()** and **printf()** are functions. As stated earlier, **main()** is the first function executed when your program begins to run. The function **printf()**, not a part of the C language proper, is a subroutine written in C. Subroutines such as this are usually written by the developer of the compiler and are a part of the standard C library. The **printf()** function causes its argument to be printed on the screen of the computer. In the HELLO program, the argument is the string in parentheses, "HELLO\n". The **\n** is the symbol C uses to denote a new line; that is, a carriage return/line feed combination.

The General Form of C Functions

The HELLO program introduces the general form of a C function. The program starts with **main()**. Then an opening brace signifies the beginning of the function followed by any statements that make up the function. In this program, the only statement is **printf( )**. The closing brace signals the end of a function. Here it also marks the end of the program. The general form of a function is

> *function __name(argument list)*
> *argument __list declaration*
>   {   *opening brace begins the body of the function*
>   .
>   .   *body of the function*
>   .
>   }   *closing brace ends the function*

As you can see, the first thing a function needs is the name. Inside the parentheses following the function name is the *list of arguments*. Immediately following on the next line is the *argument list declaration*, which tells the compiler what type of variable to expect. Next, braces surround the body of the function. The *body of the function* is composed of the C statements that define what the function does. C does have an explicit **return** statement that forces a return from a function. Since no explicit **return** is encountered, the function automatically stops execution and returns when it reaches the final brace. This differs from the BASIC **GOSUB-RETURN** combination because BASIC requires the **RETURN** to know when to return from a subroutine.

The *main( )* Function

The **main( )** function is special because it is the first function called when your program executes. It signifies the beginning of your program. Unlike a program in BASIC, which begins at the lowest line number or the "top" of the program, a C program begins with a call to the **main( )** function. The **main( )** function can be anywhere in your program, although it is generally the first function for the sake of clarity. There *must be* a **main( )** somewhere in your program so the C compiler can determine where to start execution.

The **main( )** function is just like every other C function, except that the closing brace of **main( )** signals the end of the program. When this brace is reached, the program exits to the operating system.

There can only be one **main( )** in a program. If there were more than one, your program would not know where to begin execution. Most compilers will catch an error like this before you ever reach the execution stage.

Function Arguments

In the HELLO program, the function **printf( )** has one argument: the string that will be printed on the computer screen. Functions in C can have from zero to several arguments. (The upper limit is determined by the compiler you are using.) An *argument* is a value that is passed into a function. When a function is defined, variables that will receive argument values must also be declared. These are called the *formal parameters* of the function. For example, the following function will return the product of the two integer arguments. The **return** statement transmits the product back to the calling routine.

```
mul(x,y)    /* mul function */
int x,y;            /* here x and y are declared
                       to be integer variables   */
{
        return(x*y); /* gives the product of the
                        two arguments   */
}
```

Each time **mul( )** is called, it will multiply the values of **x** and **y**. Remember, however, that **x** and **y** are simply the function's operational variables that receive the values you assign when calling the function.

Figure 2-2 presents a short program that uses the **mul( )** function. This program will print two numbers on the screen: **2** and **2340**. The variables **x**, **y**, **j**, and **k** are not modified by the call to the **mul( )** function. In fact, **x** and **y** in **main( )** have no relationship to **x** and **y** in **mul( )**.

The **mul( )** function will multiply the values of both **x** and **y** as well as **j** and **k**. When you call a function, the arguments may be either constants, as in the HELLO program, or variables, as in the **mul( )** example. When you created the function **mul( )** with two arguments, you declared the argument variables to be **x** and **y**. These are the formal parameters of the function; they hold the information that you pass in when calling the function. C copies the value of the constant or variable used as a function argument into the variable that the function has declared in its list of arguments. Unlike some other computer languages, C does not copy any information back into the function arguments.

In C functions, arguments are always separated by commas. In this book, the term *argument list* will refer to comma-separated arguments. The argument list for **mul( )** is **x,y**.

```
main()
{
        int x,y,j,k;

        x=1
        y=2;
        p=mul(x,y);
        printf("%d",p);   /* printf p in decimal */

        j=234;
        k=10;
        p=mul(k,j);
        printf("%d",p);
}

mul(x,y)   /* mul function */
int x,y;             /* here x and y are declared
                        to be integer variables  */
{
        return(x*y); /* gives the product of the
                        two arguments  */
}
```

Figure 2-2.   A program using the **mul()** function

The *printf()* Function

Every program example in this book that produces console output will use the **printf()** function. This function is a multipurpose console output function provided with your C compiler. You have already seen how to print a character string on your computer's screen in the HELLO program. The program in Figure 2-3 will print the number **123** on the screen. The BASIC equivalent is provided for comparison.

```
main()
{                                    10 PRINT 123
    printf("%d",123);                20 END
}
```

Figure 2-3.   C version and BASIC version of a program that prints **123**

In this program, **printf( )** is called with two arguments. The first argument, "**%d**", tells **printf( )** how to treat the second argument, **123**. The percent sign tells **printf( )** that the next character is a format control command indicating how the following data is to be printed. The **d** means that the following data—in this case the number 123—should be displayed as a decimal number.

The general form of **printf( )** is

printf("*control string*",*argument list*)

In the **printf( )** function, the control string contains format commands that tell **printf( )** how to display the remaining arguments on the screen and also how many other arguments there are. Remember that each argument in the argument list is separated by a comma. The **printf( )** allows a variety of format commands, as shown in Table 2-1.

The control string may contain either one or both of two types of data: characters to be printed or instructions for displaying the subsequent arguments in the argument list. Format commands may be embedded anywhere in the first string of characters. When you call **printf( )**, the control string is scanned by **printf( )**. All regular characters are simply printed on the screen as is. When a format command is encountered, **printf( )** will remember to use it when printing the appropriate argument. Format commands and

Table 2-1.   Format Control Codes of **printf( )**

printf( ) code	Format
%c	single character
%d	decimal
%e	scientific notation
%f	decimal floating point
%g	uses %e or %f, whichever is shorter
%o	octal
%s	string of characters
%u	unsigned decimal
%x	hexadecimal

Table 2-2. Examples of the **printf( )** Function

Control string and argument list	Resulting display
("%s %d", "this is a string", 100);	this is a string 100
("this is a string %d", 100);	this is a string 100
("number %d is decimal, %f is float.", 10,110.789);	number 10 is decimal, 110.789 is float
("%c %s %d−%x", 'a', "number in decimal and hex: ", 10, 10);	a number in decimal and hex: 10−A
("%s", "HELLO \n";	HELLO

arguments are matched left to right. The number of format commands in the control string tells **printf( )** how many subsequent arguments to expect.

If you wish to print a % as a character embedded in the control string, you must use two percent signs next to each other, that is, %%.

There are two things to remember about using **printf( )** to display character and string data. First, individual characters that use the **%c** format command must be enclosed between single quotes; for example, 'c'. Second, strings of characters that use the **%s** format command are enclosed between double quotes; for example, **"this is a string"**. Table 2-2 will show you the **printf( )** function in action.

You *must* have the same number of arguments as you do format commands in the control string. The format commands may also include modifiers that define decimal places and, in the case of strings, leading and trailing blanks. These and other details about the **printf( )** function will be explained in Chapter 5.

Variables in C

Although much of Chapter 3 will discuss variables and their usage, there are a few things about them that you should know now. Variable names in C can be from one character to several characters long. The C compiler that you are using will determine their maximum length; however, it is safe to assume you will have at least six characters. Variable names may start with any letter of the alphabet or an underscore character. Next there may be either a letter, a number, or the underscore. The underscore can be used to enhance the readability of a variable name, as in **first__name**. Unlike most dialects of BASIC, uppercase and lowercase letters are distinguishable when used in a variable; that is, to C, **count** and **COUNT** are separate names. Some examples of acceptable variable names are **first, last, Addr1, top__of__file, name23, __temp, t, s23e3**, and so on.

You cannot use any of the C keywords as variable names. *Keywords* are the words that make up the C programming language. You also should not call your variables by the same name as other C functions. Although your routines take precedence over other system routines and variables, calling variables by the same name as standard C functions may confuse you and some compilers. Beyond these two restrictions, good programming practice dictates that you should use variable names that reflect the meaning or usage of the variable.

In C, as in all programming languages, there are all types of variables. For example, all BASICs have string and floating point variables, and some also have integer variables. As shown in Table 2-3, C has seven built-in data types, which have C keyword equivalents. In addition to these, you can also create a group of variables called a *structure*.

Variables that are known to all functions in your program are called *global variables*. Variables that are known only to the function that uses them are called *local variables*.

All variables must be declared before they are used in C. The declaration process not only tells the compiler what the variable's name is, but also what *type* of data it is. You first specify the type of variable desired and then give the list of variables that should be of that type. For example, to declare the

Table 2-3. C Built-in Data Types and Their Keyword Equivalents

Data type	C keyword equivalent
character	char
integer	int
short integer	short int
long integer	long int
unsigned integer	unsigned int
floating point	float
double-precision floating point	double

variables **first,** **last,** and **middle** as integers, you would use the following statement:

```
int first, last, middle;
```

Variable declaration statements, like all statements in C, end in a semicolon. Remember that the term **int** is the C keyword for the integer data type.

Variables may be declared at any point in a C program. However, they are usually declared at the beginning of a function directly after the first opening brace. For example, the following declares a variable of each type:

```
sample()
{
        int count;
        char c;
        float value;
        short int top;
        long int eof_counter;
        double pay_out;
        unsigned int u;
        .
        .        /* code for the body of the
        .            function goes here */
}
```

In this example, the declared variables will be known only to the function **sample()**; they are *local* to that function. If you wish to use a variable throughout your entire program (in other words, a global variable), you must declare it *outside* of any function. For example, if you are writing a program that uses the integer variable **line — count** throughout the program, it must be declared *before* you even define **main()**:

```
int line_count;
main()
{
    .
    .
    .
}
```

C Keywords

C has 28 keywords that may not be used as variable or function names. These words, when combined with the formal C syntax, form the C programming

auto	double	if	static
break	else	int	struct
case	entry	long	switch
char	extern	register	typedef
continue	float	return	union
default	for	sizeof	unsigned
do	goto	short	while

Figure 2-4. Keyword list

language. The keywords are listed in Figure 2-4. C requires that all keywords be lowercase. For example, **RETURN** will *not* be recognized as the keyword **return**.

Semicolons, Braces, Comments, And Position

You may have been wondering why so many statements end with a semicolon. In C, the semicolon is a statement *terminator;* that is, each individual statement must end with a semicolon. It indicates the end of one logical entity. (Be careful if you know Pascal; in Pascal the semicolon is a statement *separator.*)

Remember that a block is a set of logically connected statements inside opening and closing braces. If you consider a block as a group of statements with a semicolon after each statement, it makes sense that the block itself is not followed by a separate semicolon.

Unlike BASIC, C does not recognize the end of the line as a terminator. This means C has no constraints on position, which allows you to group statements together for clarity, as shown by these two equivalent code fragments:

```
x=y;
y=y+1;
mul(x,y);
```

as a three-line group is the same as

```
x=y;   y=y+1;            mul(x,y);
```

Comments in C may be placed anywhere in a program and are enclosed between two markers. The start comment marker is /* and the end comment marker is */. Adding comments to the HELLO program could make it look like Figure 2-5.

Indentation Practices

As you may have noticed in the previous examples, certain statements are indented. The C language can have a free form because it does not matter where you place statements on a line.

However, a common and accepted indentation style has developed over the years that allows for very readable programs. This book follows that style and it is recommended that you do so as well. Using this style, you indent after each opening brace and return to the previous level brace. There are certain statements that encourage additional indenting and these will be covered later.

The Standard
C Library

In the discussion of the HELLO program of Figure 2-1, it was mentioned that **printf()** was written by the developer of the compiler. The function

```
    main()
    {
            /* this program prints the word hello on the
                computer's screen */
            printf("HELLO\n");
    }    /* this is the end of the program */
```

Figure 2-5. HELLO program with comments

printf( ) is not even part of the C language, yet you will use it in almost every C program you write. Where did it come from? It came from the *standard C library.*

All C compilers have a standard C library that provides functions to perform most common tasks. The designers of your C compiler have already written many of the general-purpose functions you will use. When you use a function not previously identified in your program, the C compiler "remembers" the function's name: part of the compiler finds the missing function and adds it to your object code. The part of the compiler that performs this process is called a *linker,* and the process is called *linking.* Some C compilers have their own linkers, and others use the standard linker supplied with your operating system.

The linking process adds code that has already been compiled into your program. The functions that are kept in the library are in *relocatable format.* This means that the memory addresses for the various machine code instructions have not been absolutely defined, but rather only offset information has been kept. When your program links with the functions in the standard library, these memory offsets are used to create the actual addresses used. There are several technical manuals and books that explain this process in more detail. However, you do not need any further understanding of the actual relocation process in order to program in C.

The phrase *standard C library* is optimistic. There is nothing in the C language that defines *exactly* which functions are going to be in a library or how they will work. The designers of each C compiler decide that. However, most commercial C compilers use *UNIX standard library functions.* C was originally developed under the UNIX operating system, and although there is no direct connection, that version of C is generally thought of as the standard implementation. (In Appendix B, you will find a list of the most common functions found in the standard C library.)

Even though some C compilers call themselves UNIX standard, the function library of each may call the standard functions by slightly different names. For example, the function to copy one string into another is generally called **strcpy( )**, but it has also been called **strcopy( )** and **stringcpy( )**. Read your user manual to find out what names are used by your compiler.

Many functions that you will need in C are already written. They act as building blocks that you simply assemble. If you write a function that you will use often, it too can be placed into a library. Some compilers will allow you to place this in the standard library; others will make you create an additional library. Either way, the code will be there for you to use over and over.

Review of Terms

Before you learn how to use your C compiler, you should review some important terms. You will find these terms in the user manual of your C compiler.

Source code. The text of a program that a user can read; commonly thought of as *the program.*

Object code. The translation of the source code of a program into machine code, which the computer can read and execute directly.

Linker. A program that links separately compiled functions into one program; the linker combines the functions in the standard C library with the code you write.

Library. The file containing the standard functions that may be used by your program. These functions include all I/O operations as well as other useful routines.

Compile time. The events that occur while your program is being compiled. A common compile-time occurrence is a syntax error.

Run time. The events that occur while your program is executing.

Compiling A C Program

The C programming language is almost always compiled. When you compile a C program, you actually follow four steps.

- Create your program.

- Compile your program.

- Link your program with whatever functions are needed from the library.

- Execute your program.

Unlike a BASIC interpreter, which has the source code editor built-in, a C compiler (or any compiler for that matter) must have a separate editor to create programs. If you are using CP/M, you can use ED, the standard CP/M editor. If you are using MS-DOS or PC-DOS, you can use EDLIN. If you are using UNIX, you can use VI. There are also numerous excellent screen editors on the market that are generally suitable as well.

Compilers only accept standard text files for input. For example, your compiler will not accept files created by certain word processors because they have control codes and nonprinting characters. If you are unsure whether your editor is suitable, ask your dealer or a knowledgeable friend.

Using Batch Commands
To Compile Your Program

Both CP/M and MS-DOS/PC-DOS allow you to define a batch command that will automatically execute a number of tasks. When working with a compiler, you can use a batch command to help with the compilation process. The %1 and the $1 hold the name of your program. The batch commands listed in Table 2-4 will compile, link, and run your program. The batch commands listed are simply guides; consult your C manual for the exact compilation sequence.

If you are using an operating system other than MS-DOS/PC-DOS or CP/M, you will have to determine if it has a batch capability.

Table 2-4. Examples of Batch Commands

CP/M	MS-DOS/PC-DOS
cc $1.c	cc %1.c
link $1,lib.c	link %1, lib.c
$1	%1

```
        main()
        {
                int a,b,c;

                printf("Enter two numbers\n");
                a=getnum();
                b=getnum();
                c=mul(a,b);
                printf("a * b = %d",c);
        }

        mul(x,y)
        int x,y;
        {
                return(x*y);
        }

        getnum()
        {
                char s[80];

                gets(s);
                return(atoi(s)); /* convert to int */
        }



        10 PRINT "Enter two numbers"
        20 INPUT A,B
        30 GOSUB 100
        40 PRINT "a * b = "; C
        50 END
        100 C = A*B
        130 RETURN
```

Figure 2-6. C and BASIC versions of a sample program using the general principles given in Chapter 2

A Sample Program

A short, sample program will be examined that illustrates the general principles that have been discussed in this chapter. By now you probably have an idea of what a C program actually looks like, and sometimes a listing is "worth a thousand words." The corresponding BASIC version is printed with it for comparison. This program, listed in Figure 2-6, will input two numbers from the keyboard and print their product on the screen.

The function **getnum()** is often found in the standard library and it will read a number typed from the keyboard. If your compiler's standard library does not have it, it has been included in this example, and you can simply make it part of your program. The **mul()** function is exactly as it was described earlier with the missing pieces added.

This sample program gives you an idea of what a C program looks like. In the C version, the function **mul()** is general; that is, it will multiply any two integer variables together, while the subroutine at line 100 of the BASIC version will multiply only **A** and **B** together. This ability to write generalized functions is one of the more important aspects of the C language.

E X E R C I S E S

1. If you haven't done so already, run the HELLO program in Figure 2-1. Confirm that you can successfully compile a program with your C compiler.

2. Write a short program that prints the following output on the screen:

```
This is line one.
This is line two.
```

3. Write **printf()** statements that will display the following on your screen:

```
This is a test. 1 2 3
123.23
These are characters: a b c
```

4. Show the declaration statements that will declare the following variables as indicated:

up, down	as integers
first, last	as single-precision floating point
c	as a character

A N S W E R S

2.
```
main()
{
      printf("This is line one.\n");
      printf("This is line two.\n");
}
```

3.
```
printf("This is a test. %d %d %d",1,2,3);

printf("%f",123.23);

printf("These are characters: %c %c %c",'a','b','c');
```

4.
```
int up, down;
float first, last;
char c;
```

Variables, Constants, Operators, And Expressions

CHAPTER 3

Variables and constants are manipulated by operators to form expressions. This is the basis of all programming. This chapter explains these concepts as they relate to the C programming language.

Variables

Variable names in C can vary from one to several characters, with the first character being a letter and subsequent characters being either letters, numbers, or the underscore character. A variable may not be the same as a C keyword, and it should not have the same name as a function that you wrote or that is already in the C library.

Data Types

As you saw in Chapter 2, there are seven built-in types of variables. The size and range of these data types vary with each processor type and with the implementation of the C compiler. For most microcomputers, the size and range information in Table 3-1 will be correct.

The ranges of **float** and **double** types are generally given in *digits of precision*. The **float** and **double** magnitudes will depend upon the method used to represent the floating point numbers. Whatever method you use, the number will be quite large.

Some implementations of C allow the modifiers **short**, **long**, and **unsigned** to be applied to data types other than **int**; for example, **unsigned double**. You should check your C compiler's user's manual to see if this is possible. Keep in mind that these additional declarations may not be supported on every C implementation and, therefore, are not portable.

In C a character is equivalent to one byte. A byte is eight bits long. In most microcomputer C implementations, a short integer is also one byte long.

In BASIC there is no concept of an unsigned number; all numbers are positive or negative. C, however, allows you to declare integers as unsigned by using the sign bit as part of the number instead of as a sign indicator. This doubles the magnitude of the largest number an integer can be. On most computers, the farthest left, or *high-order*, bit of an integer is considered to be the *sign flag*. If the sign flag is 0, the number is positive; if it is 1, the number

Table 3-1. Variable Size and Range for Microcomputers

Type	Bit Width	Range
char	8	0 to 255
int	16	−32768 to 32767
short int	8	−128 to 127
unsigned int	16	0 to 65535
long int	32	−4294967296 to 4294967295
float	32	approximately 6 digits of precision
double	64	approximately 12 digits of precision

is negative. For example, 127 in binary is

$$0\ 0\ 0\ 0\ 0\ 0\ 0\ 0\ 0\ 1\ 1\ 1\ 1\ 1\ 1\ 1$$

and −127 in binary is

$$1\ 0\ 0\ 0\ 0\ 0\ 0\ 0\ 0\ 1\ 1\ 1\ 1\ 1\ 1\ 1$$

Therefore, when you use signed numbers, as in BASIC, the largest integer may be 32,767, which looks like this in binary:

$$0\ 1\ 1\ 1\ 1\ 1\ 1\ 1\ 1\ 1\ 1\ 1\ 1\ 1\ 1\ 1$$

If the high-order bit has been set to 1, the number will be interpreted as −32,767. However, if you have declared this to be unsigned, when the high-order bit is set to 1, the number becomes 65,535.

Declaration of Variables

All C variables must be declared before they are used. The name of a variable has nothing to do with its type. The syntax for declaring each type of variable is shown in the following examples:

```
int i;
short int si;
unsigned int ui;
long int li;
float f;
double d;
```

There are three basic places in a C program where variables will be declared: inside functions, in the definition of function parameters, or outside of all functions. These variables are called local variables, formal parameters, and global variables.

Local Variables

Local variables are declared inside a function. They may be referenced only by the statements that are inside the function in which the variables are declared. Local variables are not known to other functions outside their own; for example,

```
func1()
{
        int x;

        x=10;
}
func2()
{
        int x;

        x=-199;
}
```

The integer variable **x** was declared twice, once in **func1( )** and once in **func2( )**. The **x** in **func1( )** has no bearing on and is not related to the **x** in **func2( )**.

In C, local variables are *created* when the function is called and *destroyed* when the function is exited. In a similar fashion, the storage for these local variables is created and destroyed dynamically. Although called a *dynamic variable* or *automatic variable* in some other C literature, this book will continue to use the term *local variable* when referring to variables of this sort.

Because local variables are created and destroyed with each function call, their contents are lost once the function returns. In the fragment just given, neither value of **x** will exist outside those functions. Unlike BASIC, where all variables exist all of the time, the majority of variables in most C programs are constantly being created and destroyed.

Formal Parameters

As you saw in Chapter 2, if a function has arguments, those arguments must be declared. These are called the *formal parameters* of the function. They behave like any other local variables inside the function. The declaration occurs after the function name and before the opening brace; for example,

```
func1(first, last, ch)
int first, last;
char ch;
{
    int count;
    count=first*last;
    ch='a';
       .
       .
       .
}
```

In this example **func1( )** has three arguments called **first**, **last**, and **ch**. You must tell C what type of variables these are by declaring them as shown in this fragment. After this has been done, they may be used inside the function as normal local variables. Keep in mind that, as local variables, they are also dynamic and are destroyed upon exit from the function.

You must make sure that the formal parameters you declare are the same type as the arguments you will use to call the function. If there is a type mismatch, unexpected results can occur. Unlike BASIC and most other languages, C is very robust and will generally do something, even if it is not what you want. There are few run-time errors and no bounds checking. As the programmer, you have to make sure that these errors do not occur.

As with local variables, you may make assignments to a function's formal parameters or use them in any allowable C expression, Even though these variables perform the special task of receiving the value of the arguments passed to the function, they can be used like any other local variable.

Global Variables and *extern*

You may have been wondering how to make a variable and its data stay in existence throughout the entire execution of your program. You can do this by using global variables. Unlike local variables, global variables hold their value throughout the entire time your program is running. Global variables are created by declaring them outside of any function. They may be accessed by any expression, regardless of what function that expression is in.

Consider this example:

```
int count; /*count is global */
main( )
{
    count=mul(10,123);
    .
    .
    .
}
func1( )
{
    int temp;
    temp=count;
    .
    .
    .
}
func2( )
{
    int count;
    count=10;
    .
    .
    .
}
```

You can see that the variable **count** has been declared outside of all functions. However, it could have been placed anywhere, as long as it was not in a function. Remember, though, that since you must declare a variable before you use it, it is best to declare global variables at the top of the program.

The example also shows that, while neither **main( )** nor **func1( )** has declared the variable **count**, both may use it. The **func2( )** function has, however, declared a local variable called **count**. When **func2( )** references **count**, it will be referencing only its local variable, not the global one. It is very important to remember that if a global variable and a local variable have the same name, all references to that variable name inside the function where the local variable is declared will refer only to that local variable and will have no effect on the global variable. This is usually a convenient benefit. However, if you forget this, your program can act very strangely, even though it "looks" correct.

Because C allows separately compiled modules of a large program to be linked together in order to speed up compilation, you must make sure that both files can reference the global variables. You can declare a global variable only once. If you try to declare two global variables with the same name, your C compiler will print the error message **duplicate variable name**, which means that the compiler does not know which variable you are using at any one time. The same type of problem occurs if you simply declare all your global variables in each file. You would actually be trying to create two copies of each variable. When you attempt to link your modules together, you will get the error message **duplicate label** because the linker will not know which variable to use. The solution is to declare all of your globals in one file and use **extern**-modified declarations in the other, as shown in Table 3-2.

In file two, the global variable list was copied from file one and the **extern** modifier was added to declarations. The **extern** modifier tells the compiler that the variable types and names that follow have already been declared elsewhere. In other words, **extern** lets the compiler know what the types and names are for these global variables without actually creating them again. When the linker links the two modules together, all references to the external variables are resolved.

Table 3-2. Using Global Variables in Separately Compiled Modules

```
              file one              file two
              int x, y;             extern int x, y;
              char ch;              extern char ch;
              main( )               func22( )
              {                     {
              .                         x=y/10;
              .                     }
              .                     func23( )
              }                     {
              func1( )                  y=10;
              {                     }
                  x=123
              }
```

When you use a global variable inside a function that is in the same file as the declaration for the global variable, you may elect to use **extern**, although you don't have to. For example, this is the way to use this option:

```
int first, last;        /* global definition of first and
                           last */
        main()
        {
                extern int first;   /* optional use of
                                        the extern
                                        declaration */

        }
```

Although **extern** variable declarations can occur inside the same file as the global declaration, they are not necessary there. If the C compiler comes across a variable that has not been declared, the compiler will see if it matches any of the global variables. If it does, the compiler will assume that is the variable being referenced.

In most C implementations, storage for global variables is in a fixed region of memory set aside by the C compiler. Global variables are very helpful when the same data is used in many functions in your program. However, you should avoid using unnecessary global variables for three reasons: (1) they take up memory during the entire time your program is executing, not just when they are needed; (2) using a global where a local variable will do makes your function less general because it relies on something that must be defined outside itself; and (3) using a large number of global variables can lead to program errors because of unknown, and unwanted, side effects. In BASIC, where all variables are global, a major problem in developing large programs is the accidental changing of a variable value because it was used elsewhere in the program. This can happen in C if you use too many global variables in your programs.

One of the principal points of a structured language is the compartmentalization of code and data. In C, compartmentalization is achieved through the use of local variables and functions. For example, Table 3-3 shows two ways to write **mul( )**.

Both functions will return the product of the variables **x** and **y**. However, the generalized, or *parameterized*, version can be used to return the product of *any* two numbers, whereas the specific version can be used to find the product of only the global variables **x** and **y**.

Table 3-3. Two Ways to Write **mul( )**

General	Specific
	int x,y;
mul(x,y)	mul( )
int x,y;	{
{	extern x,y;
return(x∗y);	return(x∗y);
}	}

The *static* Variables

The **static** variables are permanent variables within either their own function or file. They differ from global variables because, while they are not known outside their function or file, they maintain their values between calls. This feature can make them very useful when you write generalized functions and function libraries that are used by other programmers.

A good example of a function that might require such a variable is a number-series generator that produces a new number based on the last one. It would be possible for you to declare a global variable for this value each time the function is used, but you must remember to do it every time, which is a major drawback. Using a global variable would make this function difficult to place in a function library. The solution is to declare the variable that holds the generated number to be **static**, as shown:

```
series()
{
        static int series_num;

        series_num=series_num+23;
        return(series_num);
}
```

In this example, the variable **series-num** stays in existence between function calls instead of coming and going the way a normal local variable would. This means that each call to **series( )** can produce a new member of the series based on the last number without declaring that variable globally.

You may have noticed something unusual about the function **series( )** as it stands in the example. The static variable **series—num** is never initialized to a known value. This means that the first time the function is called, **series— num** will have some random value. While this is acceptable for some applications, most series generators will need a well-defined starting point. One solution would be to initialize **series—num** prior to the first call to **series( )**, which is easily done if **series—num** were a global variable. However, this solution would make it difficult to put the function **series( )** into a library for general use. The better solution is to use **static** global variables.

Let's rewrite the series generation example so that the starting value can be initialized by a call to the function **series—start( )**. The example now looks like this:

```
static int series_num;
series()
{
        series_num=series_num+23;
        return(series_num);
}

series_start(seed)
int seed;
{
        series_num=seed;
}
```

Calling **series—start( )** with some known integer value initializes the series generator. After that, calls to **series( )** will generate the next element in the series.

At this point you may be asking, If global variables stay in existence throughout the execution of a program, why was **series—num** made **static**? Isn't the function **series( )** unusable for placement in a library for general use? The answers to these questions hinge on a side benefit of **static**.

Remember that the names of local **static** variables are known only to the function in which they are declared and the names of global **static** variables are known only to the file in which they reside. This means that if you place the **series( )** and the **series—start( )** functions in a library, you can use the functions, but you cannot reference the variable **series—num**. It is hidden from you. In fact, you may even declare and use another variable called **series—**

num in your program (in another file, of course) and not cause any problems. In essence, the **static** modifier allows variables to exist that are known to the functions that need them without confusing other functions.

The **static** variables allow you, the programmer, to hide portions of your program from other portions. This can be a tremendous advantage when you are trying to manage a very large and complex program. Using the **static** modifier lets you create very general functions that can go into libraries for later use.

The *register* Variables

C has one last variable/declaration modifier that applies only to type **int** and **char** in most cases. The **register** modifier forces the C compiler to keep the value of variables declared with this modifier in the *register* of the CPU rather than in memory, where normal variables are stored. This means that operations on **register** variables can occur much faster than those on variables stored in memory because the value of **register** variables are held in the CPU and do not require a memory access. This makes **register** variables ideal for loop control. The **register** modifier can apply only to local variables and to the formal parameters in a function definition. Global **register** variables are disallowed. Here is an example of how to declare **register** variables of **int** and **char**:

```
func1(s,u)
register int s;
register char u;
{
    float temp;
    register int counter;
    .
    .
    .
}
```

The exact number of **register** variables within any one function is determined by both the processor type and the specific implementation of C that you are using. For most 8-bit systems, only one **register** variable is allowed. For 16-bit systems, usually two or more **register** variables may be used. You will only need to worry about this when speed is a concern because if you have declared too many **register** variables, the C compiler will automatically make them into nonregister variables. Throughout this book most loop-control variables will be of type **register**.

Arrays

Although Chapter 8 will explain arrays in detail, some important concepts need to be noted now. *Arrays* can be of any variable type. The general form of the array declaration is

type variable—name[number of elements];

For example, to make an array called **q** with ten integer elements, you would write

```
int q[10];
```

Array elements are referenced by specifying the element number in brackets after the array name. To reference the first three elements of array **q**, you would write

```
q[0]
q[1]
q[2]
```

Unlike some BASICs, all arrays in C start with element zero. This means that the ten elements of array **q** are indexed from zero to nine.

C performs no bounds checking, so it is your responsibility to make sure that your array indexes are within the scope you have declared. If you exceed that scope, you will destroy either the contents of other variables or the actual code to your program, either of which may have devastating results.

Character strings are simply arrays of characters in C. The program in Figure 3-1 reads in a string of characters, prints them, and then prints only the first three characters. (The equivalent BASIC program is also shown.) The C version uses **gets( )**, a function usually found in C libraries, which will read a string of characters from the keyboard and place them into a character array.

Remember that you can call **printf( )** and **gets( )** by simply using the name of the string variable without any indexes when you mean the entire string.

```
main()
{
    char string[80]; /* declare an array of chars 80
                        characters long */
    gets(string); /* use a routine from the C library to
                     get a string from the keyboard */
    printf(string); /* print out the string */
    /* now print the first three characters */
    printf("%c %c %c",string[0],string[1],string[2]);
}

10 INPUT A$
20 PRINT A$
30 PRINT MID$(A$,1,1);MID$(A$,2,1);MID$(A$,3,1);
40 END
```

Figure 3-1. C and BASIC versions of a program that reads and prints a character string and then prints only the first three characters

Assignment Statements

Up to this point, the examples have been assigning variables values without discussion. This section will explain the general assignment process and syntax, as well as some variations.

The general form of the *assignment statement* is

$$variable\_name = expression;$$

where an expression may be as simple as a constant or as complex as an expression. Like BASIC and FORTRAN, C uses a single equal sign to indicate assignment. (Pascal uses the := construct.) The *target*, or left part, of the assignment must be a variable, not a function or a constant.

Type Conversion in Assignments

Type conversion refers to the situation in which variables of one type are mixed with variables of another type. When this occurs in an assignment statement, the type conversion rule is very easy: the value of the right side of the assignment is converted to the type of the left side, the target variable. For example,

```
int x;
char ch;
float    f;

func()
{
        ch=x;
        x=f;
        f=ch;
        f=x;
}
```

In **ch**=**x**, the left high-order bits of the integer variable **x** are lopped off leaving **ch** with the lower 8 bits. If **x** was between 256 and 0 to begin with, **ch** and **x** would have identical values. Otherwise, the value of **ch** would reflect only the lower-order bits of **x**. In **x**=**f**, **x** will receive the nonfractional part of **f**. In **f**=**ch**, **f** will convert the 8-bit integer value stored in **ch** to the same value except in the floating-point format. This also happens in **f**=**x**, except that **f** will convert an integer value into floating-point format.

When converting from integers to characters, long integers to integers, and integers to short integers, the basic rule to remember is that the appropriate amount of high-order bits will be removed. This means 8 bits will be lost when going from an integer to a character or short integer, and 16 bits will be lost when going from a long integer to an integer.

Table 3-4 synopsizes these assignment type conversions. You must remember two important points:

1. The conversion of an **int** to a **float**, or a type **float** to **double**, will not add any precision or accuracy. These kinds of conversions will only change the form in which the value is represented.

2. Some C compilers (and processors) will always treat a **char** variable as positive, regardless of what value it has when converting it to an **int** or **float**. Other compilers will treat values of **char** variables greater than 127 as negative numbers when converting. Generally speaking, you should use **char** variables for characters and use **int** variables when needed to avoid a possible problem in this area.

To use Table 3-4 to make a conversion not directly shown, simply convert

Table 3-4. Assignment Type Conversion Rules

Target Type	Expression Type	Possible Information Loss
char	short int	sign
char	int	high-order 8 bits
char	long int	high-order 24 bits
short int	int	high-order 8 bits
short int	long int	high-order 24 bits
int	long int	high-order 16 bits
int	float	fractional part and possibly more
float	double	precision; result rounded

down until you finish. For example, to convert from **double** to an **int**, first convert from a **double** to **float**, and then from a **float** to an **int**.

If you have used a computer language like Pascal, which prohibits this automatic type conversion, you may think that C is very loose and sloppy. However, keep in mind that C was designed to make the life of the programmer easier by allowing work to be done in C rather than assembler. To replace assembler, C has to allow such type conversions.

Variable and Array Initialization

You can give most variables in C a value at the same time they are declared by placing an equal sign and a constant after the variable name. The general form of initialization is

type variable_name = constant;

Some examples are

```
char ch = 'a';
int first = 0;
float balance = 123.23;
```

Global and **static** variables are initialized only at the beginning of the program. Local and **register** variables are initialized each time the function is entered. All global and **static** variables are supposed to be initialized to zero if no other initializer is specified, but don't count on this because it is a commonly overlooked detail when C compilers are implemented. Local and **register** values that are not initialized will have unknown values before the first assignment is made to them.

You may also initialize global arrays. For character arrays used to hold strings, you may enclose the string in quotes. A *string* is an array of characters terminated by a null. A *null* in C is usually a 0. However, because this can change from implementation to implementation, you should use the special **\0** symbol for the null. Strings in your program text will have the null terminator placed at the end automatically by the C compiler so you do not need to do it. For example, to initialize the array **str** with the string "**Hi there**", you could write

```
char str[9] = "Hi there";
```

The reason that **str** had to be nine elements long is that all strings in C are terminated by a null, which is automatically appended by the C compiler.

When you printed the string **HELLO** on your screen in Chapter 2, you were using a string constant. The length of the string **HELLO** is not five, but rather six because of the null terminator, which you don't see. This is important when you declare character arrays that will hold strings. You need to declare them one character larger than the maximum number of characters you wish them to hold to allow room for the null terminator.

Arrays may also be initialized by listing their elements, separated by commas, between braces. For example, to initialize "**Hi there**" by this method, you could write

```
char str[9] = {'H','i',' ','t','h','e','r','e','\0'};
```

The '\0' stands for the null at the end of a string. You must use it explicitly here because the C compiler does not know that this is a character string.

One last point: local arrays may not be initialized; however, local **static** arrays can be.

Constants

Constants in C refer to fixed values that may not be altered by a program. They can be of any data type, as shown in Table 3-5.

Table 3-5. Examples of Constants

Data Type	Constant Examples
char	'a' '\n' '9'
int	1 123 21000 -234
long int	35000 -34
short int	10 -12 90
unsigned int	10000 987
float	123.23 4.34e-3
double	123.23 12312333 -0.9876324

C supports one other type of constant in addition to those of the seven predefined data types. This is a string constant. All string constants are enclosed between double quotes, such as **"this is a test"**. You must not confuse strings with characters. A single character constant is enclosed with single quotes, such as '**a**'. Remember that all strings end with a null.

Backslash Character Constants

Enclosing all character constants in single quotes works for most printing characters, but a few—such as the carriage return—are impossible to enter from the keyboard. For this reason, C has created the special backslash character constants.

The symbol '**\n**' stands for newline and the '**\0**' stands for the null terminator. C supports several special backslash codes, as listed in Table 3-6, that enable you to enter these special characters as constants. You should use the backslash codes instead of their ASCII equivalents to help ensure portability.

Operators

C is very rich in built-in operators. An *operator* is a symbol that tells the compiler to perform specific mathematical or logical manipulations. C has

Table 3-6. Backslash Codes

Code	Meaning
\b	backspace
\f	form feed
\n	newline
\r	carriage return
\t	horizontal tab
\'	single quote character
\0	null

three classes of operators: *arithmetic, relational and logical,* and *bitwise.* In addition, C has some special operators.

Arithmetic Operators

Table 3-7 lists the arithmetic operators allowed in C. The operators +, −, *, and / all work the same way in C as they do in BASIC or any other computer language. These can be applied to any built-in data type allowed by C. When

Table 3-7. Arithmetic Operators

Operator	Action
−	subtraction; also unary minus
+	addition
*	multiplication
/	division
%	modulo division
−−	decrement
++	increment

/ is applied to an integer or character, any remainder will be truncated; for example, 10/3 will equal 3 in integer division.

The unary minus, in effect, multiplies its single operand by -1. Therefore, any number preceded by a minus sign switches its sign.

In C, the modulo division operator % works the same way that it does in other languages. Remember that the modulo division operation yields the remainder of an integer division. However, as such, % cannot be used on type **float** or **double**. This is an example of the use of %:

```
int x,y;

x=10;
y=3;
printf("%d",x/y);    /* will display 3 */
printf("%d",x%y);    /* will display 1, the remainder of
                        the integer division */
x=1;
y=2;
printf("%d %d", x/y, x%y); /* will display 0 1 */
```

The last line prints a 0 and 1 because 1/2 in integer division is 0 with a remainder of 1; therefore, 1%2 yields the remainder 1.

C allows two very useful operators not generally found in other computer languages. These are the *increment* and *decrement* operators: $++$ and $--$. The operation $++$ adds 1 to its operand, and $--$ subtracts 1. Therefore, the following are equivalent operations:

$$x=x+1; \text{ is the same as } ++x;$$
$$x=x-1; \text{ is the same as } --x;$$

Both the increment and decrement operators may either precede or follow the operand. For example,

$$x=x+1;$$

can be written as either

$$++x;$$

or

$$x++;$$

There is, however, a difference when they are used in an expression. When an increment or decrement operator precedes its operand, C will perform the operation prior to using the operand's value. If the operator follows its operand, C will use the operand's value before incrementing or decrementing it. Consider the following:

```
x=10;
y=++x;
```

In this case, **y** will be set to 11. However, if this had been written

```
x=10;
y=x++;
```

y would have been set to 10. In both cases, **x** is still set to 11; the difference is when the change in value occurs. There are significant advantages in being able to control when the increment or decrement operation takes place.

Most C compilers write very fast, efficient object code for increment and decrement operations that is better than the code generated by using an assignment statement. Hence, it is a good idea to use increment and decrement operators when you can.

Table 3-8 lists the precedence of the arithmetic operators. Operators on the same precedence level are evaluated by the compiler from left to right. Of course, parentheses may be used to alter the order of evaluation. Parentheses are treated by C in the same way they are by virtually all other computer languages: they force an operation, or set of operations, to have a higher precedence level.

Table 3-8. Precedence of Arithmetic Operations

highest	++ --
	- (unary minus)
	* / %
lowest	+ -

Relational and Logical Operators

In the terms *relational operator* and *logical operator, relational* refers to the relationships that values have with one another, and *logical* refers to the ways these relationships can be connected together. Because the relational and logical operators often work together, they will be discussed together here.

The key to the concepts of relational and logical operators is the idea of true and false. In C, true is any value other than 0; false is 0. Therefore, expressions that use relational or logical operators will return 1 for true and 0 for false.

Table 3-9 shows the relational and logical operators. If you know BASIC, you should note that there are differences between C and BASIC. For example, *not equal* in C is !=, while in BASIC it is <>; and the check for equality is the double equal sign, ==, not the single equal sign as used in BASIC. Note also that the logical operators are different: C uses the special operators &&, ||, and !.

Both the relational and logical operators have lower precedence than the arithmetic operators. This means that an expression like 10 > 1+12 is evaluated as if it were written 10 > (1+12). The result is, of course, false. Another

Table 3-9. Relational and Logical Operators

Relational Operator	Action
>	greater than
>=	greater than or equal
<	less than
<=	less than or equal
==	equal
!=	not equal

Logical Operator	Action
&&	AND
||	OR
!	NOT

example is the expression

```
10>5 && ! (10<9) || 3<=4
```

which will evaluate true. Table 3-10 shows the relative precedence of the relational and logical operators.

Remember, all relational and logical expressions produce a result of either 0 or 1. Therefore, this program fragment is not only correct, but will also print the number 1 on the display:

```
int x;

x=100;
printf("%d", x>10);
```

Bitwise Operators

Unlike many other languages, C supports a complete set of bitwise operators. Since C is designed to take the place of assembly language for most programming tasks, C must support all operations that can be done in assembler. *Bitwise operations* refers to the testing, setting, or shifting of the actual bits in an integer or character variable. These operations may *not* be used on type **float** or **double**. Table 3-11 lists these operators.

Bitwise operations most often find application in device drivers—modem programs, disk file routines, and printer routines—because the bitwise operations can be used to mask off certain bits, such as parity. (The parity bit

Table 3-10. Precedence of Relational and Logical Operators

highest	!
	> >= < <=
	== !=
	&&
lowest	||

Table 3-11. The Bitwise Operators

Operator	Action
&	AND
|	OR
^	exclusive OR
~	one's complement
>>	shift right
<<	shift left

is used to confirm that the rest of the bits in the byte are unchanged. It is always the high-order bit in each byte.)

You can think of the bitwise **AND** as a way to turn bits off. By using **AND**, any bit that is 0 in either operand will cause the corresponding bit in the variable to be set to 0. For example, the following function will read a character from the modem port using the function **read_modem( )** and resets the parity bit to zero:

```
char ch;

get_char_from_modem()
{
        ch=read_modem(); /* get a character from the
                            modem port */
        return(ch & 127);
}
```

Parity is indicated by the eighth bit, which is set to zero by ANDing it with a byte that has bits 1 through 7 set to 1 and bit 8 set to 0. The expression **ch & 127** means to **AND** together the bits in **ch** with the bits that make up the number 127. The net result is that the eighth bit of **ch** will be set to 0. In the following example, assume that **ch** had received the character 'A' and had the parity bit set.

```
      parity bit
        1 1 0 0 0 0 0 1   ch containing an 'A' with parity set
    &   0 1 1 1 1 1 1 1   127 in binary
        ───────────────   do bitwise AND
        0 1 0 0 0 0 0 1   'A' without parity
```

The bitwise **OR** can be used to turn bits on. Any bit that is set to 1 in either operand will cause the corresponding bit in the variable to be set to 1. For example, this is **128 | 3**:

```
    1 0 0 0 0 0 0 0   128 in binary
    0 0 0 0 0 0 1 1   3 in binary
|   _____  bitwise OR
    1 0 0 0 0 0 1 1   result
```

An exclusive OR, usually abbreviated XOR, will set a bit on only if the bits being compared are different. For example, **127 ^ 120** is

```
    0 1 1 1 1 1 1 1   127 in binary
    0 1 1 1 1 0 0 0   120 in binary
^   _____  bitwise XOR
    0 0 0 0 0 1 1 1   result
```

In general, bitwise ANDs, ORs, and XORs apply their operations directly to each bit in the variable individually. For this reason and others, bitwise operations are usually not used in conditional statements in the way that the relational and logical operators are. For example, if x=7, then x **&&** 8 evaluates to true, or 1, whereas x **&** 8 evaluates to false, or 0.

Relational and logical operators always produce a result that is either 0 or 1; similar bitwise operations alter the variable in accordance with the specific operation. In other words, bitwise operations are used to change the value of variables, not to evaluate true or false conditions.

The *shift operators*, >> and <<, move all bits in a variable to the right or left as specified. The general form of the shift right statement is

variable >> number of bit positions

and the shift left statement

variable << number of bit positions

As bits are shifted off one end, zeros are brought in the other end. (On some computers, ones are shifted in, so check your C compiler's user's manual for specific details.) Remember that a shift is *not* a rotate; that is, the bits shifted off one end *do not* come back around to the other. The bits shifted off are lost, and zeros are brought in.

Table 3-12. Effects of Multiplication and Division With Shift Operators

char x;	x as each statement executes	Value of x
x=7;	0 0 0 0 0 1 1 1	7
x << 1;	0 0 0 0 1 1 1 0	14
x << 3;	0 1 1 1 0 0 0 0	112
x << 2;	1 1 0 0 0 0 0 0	192
x >> 1;	0 1 1 0 0 0 0 0	96
x >> 2;	0 0 0 1 1 0 0 0	24

Bitwise-shift operations can be very useful when decoding external device input, such as D/A convertors, and reading status information. The bitwise-shift operators can also be used to perform very fast multiplication and division of integers. A shift left will effectively multiply a number by 2 and a shift right will divide it by 2, as shown in Table 3-12. It is assumed that zeros are shifted in, while the bits shifted off the end are lost.

The one's complement operator, $\sim$, will reverse the state of each bit in the specified variable; that is, all 1's are set to 0, and all 0's are set to 1.

The bitwise operators are used often in cipher routines. If you wished to make a disk file appear unreadable, you could perform some bitwise manipulations on it. One of the simplest methods would be to complement each byte by using the one's complement to reverse each bit in the byte as shown:

original byte	0 0 1 0 1 1 0 0
after 1st complement	1 1 0 1 0 0 1 1
after 2nd complement	0 0 1 0 1 1 0 0

Notice that a sequence of two complements in a row will always produce the original number. Hence the first complement would represent the coded version of that byte; and the second complement would decode it to its original value.

To encode a file using the one's complement operator, you could use the **encode( )** function:

```
encode(ch)        /* a simple cipher function */
char ch;
{
    ch=~ch; /* complement it */
    return(ch);
}
```

The ? Operator

C allows a very powerful and convenient operator that can be used to replace statements of the if-then-else form. The ternary operator pair ?: takes the general form

$$Exp1 \; ? \; Exp2 : Exp3$$

where Exp1, Exp2, and Exp3 are expressions.

The ? operator works like this: Exp1 is evaluated. If it is true, Exp2 is evaluated and becomes the value of the expression. If Exp1 is false, Exp3 is evaluated and its value becomes the value of the expression. For example, consider

```
x=10;
y= x>9 ? 100 : 200;
```

In this example, **y** will be assigned the value 100. If **x** had been less than 9, **y** would have received the value 200. The same code written in BASIC would look like this:

```
10 X=10
20 IF X>9 THEN GOSUB 100 ELSE GOSUB 200
30 END
100 X=100
110 RETURN
200 X=200
210 RETURN
```

The ? operator will be discussed more fully in Chapter 4 in relationship to the if-then statement in C.

*The & and * Pointer Operators*

In C, a *pointer* is the memory address of a variable. Knowing a variable's address can be of great help in certain types of routines. However, pointers have two main functions in C: first, they can provide a very fast means of referencing array elements and, second, they allow C functions to modify their calling parameters. These topics and uses will be more fully explained in Chapter 7, which is devoted exclusively to pointers. For now though, you will be learning about the two special operators that allow pointers to exist.

The first operator is **&**. It is a unary operator that returns the memory address of its operand. (Remember that a unary operator only requires one operand.) For example,

```
m = &count;
```

places into **m** the memory address of the variable **count**. This address is the computer's internal location of the variable. It has nothing to do with the *value* of **count**.

Assume the variable **count** uses memory location 2000 to store its value and that it has a value of 100. Then, after the assignment **m=&count**, **m** will have the value 2000.

The second operator is *****. It is a unary operator that returns the value of the variable located at the address that follows. For example, if **m** contains the memory address of the variable **count**, then

```
q = *m;
```

will place the value of count into q. Following through with this example, q will have the value 100 because 100 is stored at location 2000, which is the memory address that was stored in m.

Unfortunately, the bitwise AND and the "address of" sign are the same and the multiplication sign and the "at location x" sign are the same. These operators have no relationship to each other. Both **&** and ***** have a higher precedence than all other arithmetic operators except the unary minus, with which they are equal.

Variables that will hold memory addresses, or pointers, as they are called in C, must be declared by putting a ***** in front of the variable name to indicate to the compiler that it will hold a pointer to that type of variable. For exam-

```
        main()      /* assignment with * and & */
        {
                int target, source;
                int *m;
                source = 10;
                m=&source;
                target=*m;
        }
```

Figure 3-2. A program that uses the * and & operators

ple, to declare a pointer-type variable for a **char ch**, you would write

```
char *ch;
```

You can mix both pointer and nonpointer directives in the same declaration statement. For example,

```
int x,*y,count;
```

will declare **x** and **count** to be integer types and **y** to be a pointer to an integer type.

In the program in Figure 3-2, the **&** and * operators are used to put the value 10 into a variable called target.

Precedence Summary

Table 3-13 lists the precedence of all C operators, including a few that will be discussed later in this book. Notice that all operators, except the unary operators and **&**, associate from left to right. The unary operators (*, **&**, −), and the **&:** operator associate from right to left.

Expressions

Operators, constants, and variables are the constituents of *expressions*. An expression in C is any valid combination of those pieces. You probably already know the general form of expressions from your other programming

Table 3-13. Precedence of C Operators

highest	( ) [ ] − → .
	! ~ ++ −− − (type) * & sizeof
	* / %
	+ −
	<< >>
	< <= > >=
	== !=
	&
	^
	|
	&&
	||
	?:
	= += −= *= /=
lowest	,

experience. A few aspects of expressions that relate specifically to C will be discussed now.

Type Conversion in Expressions

When constants and variables of different types are mixed in an expression, they are converted to the same type. The C compiler will convert all operands to the type of the largest operand. This is done on an operation-by-operation basis following these type conversion rules:

1. All **char**s and **short int**s are converted to **int**s. All **float**s are converted to **double**s.

2. For all operand pairs: if one of the operands is **double**, the other operand is converted to **double**. Otherwise, if one of the operands is **long**, the other operand is converted to **long**; or if one of the operands is **unsigned**, the other is converted to **unsigned**.

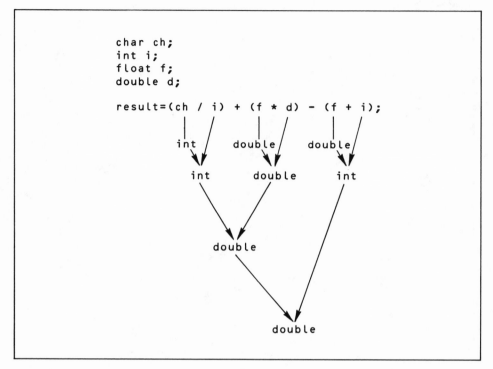

Figure 3-3. An example of type conversion

Once these conversion rules have been applied, each pair of operands will be of the same type, and the result of each operation will be the same as the type of both operands. Note that Rule 2 has several conditions that must be applied in sequence.

For example, consider the type conversions that occur in Figure 3-3. First, the character **ch** is converted to an integer and **float f** is converted to **double**. Then the outcome of **ch/i** is converted to a **double** because **f∗d** is **double**. The final result is **double** because, by this time, both operands are **double**.

```
main() /* print i and i/2 with fractions */
{
        int i;
        for(i=1; i<=100; ++t )
           printf("%d / 2 is: %f",i,(float) i /2);
}
```

Figure 3-4. A program using a cast

Casts

It is possible to force an expression to be of a specific type by using a construct called a *cast*. The general form of a cast is

(type) expression

where **type** is one of the standard C data types. For example, if you wished to make sure the expression **x/2** was evaluated to type **float**, you could write it as follows:

```
(float) x/2
```

Casts are often considered operators. As an operator, a cast is unary and has the same precedence as any other unary operator.

Although casts are not usually used much in programming, there are times when they can be very useful. For example, Figure 3-4 shows a program you would write to use an integer for loop control, yet to perform a computation on it requires a fractional part. Without the cast (**float**), only an integer division would have been performed; but the cast ensures that the fractional part of the answer will be displayed on the screen.

Spacing and Parentheses

You may add tabs and spaces to an expression in C to aid readability. For example, the next two expressions are the same.

```
x=10/y~(127/x);
x = 10 / y ~(127/x);
```

Use of redundant or additional parentheses will not cause errors or slow the execution of the expression. You are encouraged to use parentheses to make clear the exact order of evaluation, both for yourself and for others who may have to figure out your program later. For example, which of the following two expressions is easier to read?

```
x=y/3-34*temp&127;
x=(y/3) - ((34*temp) & 127);
```

C Shorthand

C has a special shorthand that simplifies the coding of a certain type of assignment statement. For example,

```
x=x+10;
```

can be written in C shorthand as

```
x+=10;
```

The operator pair += tells the compiler to assign to **x** the value of **x** plus **10**. This shorthand will work for all operators in C. The general form is

variable = variable operator expression

This is the same as

variable operator = expression

As another example,

```
x=x-100;
```

is the same as

```
x-=100;
```

You will see shorthand notation used widely in professional C programs and you should become familiar with it.

E X E R C I S E S

1. List the seven built-in data types in C.

2. List the data types that may have the **register** modifier preceding them.

3. Write a function called **add()** that has two integer arguments. The function will return the value of the sum of these two arguments.

4. Imagine a pair of functions that operate on a global variable. This global variable is called **counter**. The function **func1()** will increment **counter**, and **func2()** will decrement it. Show one way to write these two functions, assuming they are both in the same file.

5. Rewrite the functions from Exercise 4 as if they were in separate files.

6. Add to the functions from Exercise 4 a third function called **init()** that will first assign **counter** the value of 0. Put all these functions in one file and write them so they can be placed in a library.

7. Evaluate the following expressions, indicating which ones are true or false:

   a. $10==9+1$
   b. 10 **&&** 8
   c. $8 \parallel 0$
   d. 0 **&&** 0
   e. let $x=10$ and $y=9$;
       $x>= 8$ **&&** $y<=x$

8. Given the binary bit pattern, show the binary outcome of a one's complement.

$$0\ 1\ 0\ 0\ 1\ 1\ 1\ 0$$

9. Perform a bitwise AND with these binary numbers:

$$0\ 1\ 0\ 0\ 1\ 1\ 0\ 1$$
$$1\ 1\ 0\ 0\ 1\ 1\ 1\ 0$$

10. What value will count have after the execution of this code:

```
int x,*y,count;

func()
{
      x=100;
      count=999;
      y=&x;
      count=*y;
}
```

A N S W E R S

1. char
   int
   short int
   long int
   unsigned int
   float
   double

2. char and int

3.
```
add (x,y)
int x,y;
{
     return(x+y);
}
```

4.
```
int counter;

func1()
{
     counter++;
}

func2()
{
     counter--;
}
```

5. File 1:

```
int counter;

func1()
{
     counter++;
}
```

File 2:

```
extern int counter;

func2()
{
     counter--;
}
```

6.
```
static int counter;

func1()
{
     counter++;
}

func2()
{
     counter--;
}

init()
{
     counter=0;
}
```

7. *a*. true   *d*. false
   b. true   *e*. true
   c. true

8. 1 0 1 1 0 0 0 1

9. 0 1 0 0 1 1 0 0

10. 100

Program
Control
Statements

CHAPTER 4

This chapter introduces the various program control statements that C supports. These include the conditional statements **if** and **switch** and the loop constructs **while**, **for**, and **do/while**.

Conditional Statements

C supports two types of conditional statements: the **if** and the **switch** statements. In Chapter 3 you learned about the ? operator, which can perform a specific type of condition test. The ? operator is an alternative to the **if** statement in certain circumstances. Both will be discussed in this chapter. The **if** statement in C is very much like the **IF-THEN** statement in BASIC. The **switch** statement is somewhat similar to **ON-GOTO** in BASIC.

The *if* Statement

The general form of the **if** statement is

> if(test condition) statement1
> else statement2

where the objects of **if** and **else** are single statements. The **else** statement is optional. The objects of both **if** and **else** can be blocks of statements. The general form of the **if** with blocks of statements as objects is

> if (test condition)
> {
>   statements /* block1 */
> }
> else
> {
>   statements /* block2 */
> }

If the condition is true (that is, anything other than 0), **statement1** or **block1** will be executed; otherwise, if either exists, **statement2** or **block2**

```
main()  /* magic number program */
{
    int magic = 123; /* magic number */
    int guess;

    guess = getnum(); /* read an integer from the keyboard */

    if (guess == magic) printf("** Right **");
}
10 M=123
20 INPUT G
30 IF M=G THEN PRINT "** Right **"
40 END
```

Figure 4-1. Magic Number Program in C and BASIC

will be executed. Remember only one statement or block will be executed, not both.

For example, Figure 4-1 shows the C and BASIC versions of a program that prints the message ** **Right** ** when you guess the magic number. This program will be referred to as the "Magic Number Program" in later discussions.

This program uses the relational operator == to determine whether the guess entered matches the magic number. If it does, the message is printed on the screen.

The **getnum( )** function returns an integer number, which is typed in from the keyboard. The **getnum( )** function is found in many C compilers' standard libraries. If it is not in yours, you can use the one shown here and include it as part of your program when needed.

```
getnum()
{
        char    s[80];

        gets (s,80);
        return (atoi(s));
}
```

Figure 4-2 shows the Magic Number Program with an added step that prints a message when the wrong number is picked.

```
main() /* magic number program - improvement 1 *///
{

    int magic = 123; /* magic number *///
    int guess;

    guess = getnum(); /* read an integer from the keyboard */
    if (guess == magic) printf("** Right **");
    else printf(".. Wrong ..");//
}

10 M = 123
20 INPUT G
30 IF M=G THEN PRINT "** Right **" ELSE PRINT ".. Wrong ..."//
40 END
```

Figure 4-2. A version of the Magic Number in C and BASIC Program that prints error messages

A further improvement is to provide the player with a clue as to how close each guess is to the magic number. The version in Figure 4-3 uses blocks of statements as objects of the **if** and **else** statements. Remember, depending on whether you enter the magic number or not, one and only one of the blocks will be executed.

One of the most confusing aspects of **if** statements in any programming language are nested **if**s. A *nested* **if** is an **if** statement that is the object of either an **if** or an **else**. If you thought you saw one in Figure 4-3, you were right: the outer **else** block contains an **if-else** combination. Because the inner

```
main()   /* magic number program improvement 2 */
{
    int magic = 123;   /* magic number */
    int guess;

    guess = getnum();   /* read an integer from the keyboard*/
    if (guess == magic)
    {
        printf("** Right **");
        printf("%d is the magic number",magic);
    }
    else
    {
        printf(".. Wrong ..");
        if(guess > magic) printf("Too high");
        else printf("Too low");
    }
}

10 M=123
20 INPUT G
30 IF M=G THEN GOSUB 100 ELSE GOSUB 200
40 END
100 PRINT "** Right ** "; M; "is the magic number"
110 RETURN
200 PRINT ".. Wrong .."
210 IF G > M THEN PRINT "Too high" ELSE PRINT "Too low"
220 RETURN
```

Figure 4-3. Another version of the Magic Number Program in C (using blocks of statements) and in BASIC

if is contained in a block, there is no confusion about its function or execution. However, in the following:

```
if(x)
    if(y) statement1;
    else statement2;
```

which **if** does the **else** refer to? In C the **else** is linked to the closest **if** that does not have an **else** statement. In this case, the **else** is associated with the **if(y)** statement. If you want the **else** to be associated to the **if(x)**, you must use braces to force a different evaluation; for example,

```
if(x)
{
    if(y) statement1;
}
else statement2;
```

The **else** is now associated with the **if(x)** because it is no longer part of the **if** object block. In essence, the **if** and the **else** are on the same level.

The *if-else-if* Ladder

A common programming construct is the **if-else-if** ladder. It looks like this:

```
if (condition)
    statement;
else if (condition)
    statement;
else if (condition)
    statement;
    .
    .
    .
else
    statement;
```

The conditions are evaluated from the top downward. As soon as a true condition is found, the statement associated with it is executed, and the rest of the ladder is bypassed. If none of the conditions are true, the final **else** will be executed. The final **else** often acts as a *default condition*; that is, if all

```
main()   /* magic number program version 3 */
{
     int magic = 123;   /* magic number */
     int guess

     guess = getnum();   /* read an integer from the keyboard */
     if (guess == magic)
     {
          printf("** Right **");
          printf("%d is the magic number",magic);
     }
     else if(guess > magic)
          printf(".. Wrong .. Too High");
     else printf(".. Wrong .. Too Low");
}
```

Figure 4-4. Magic Number Program with an **if-else-if** ladder

other conditional tests fail, the last **else** statement is performed. If the final **else** is not present, no action will take place if all other conditions are false.

Figure 4-4 shows what the Magic Number Program would look like using an **if-else-if** ladder.

The ? Alternative

One final method of writing the Magic Number Program involves the ? operator. As you remember from Chapter 3, the ? operator evaluates one of two expressions based on the truth of its conditional expression. When a function is part of an expression, it is executed in order to derive its value. You could write a version of the Magic Number Program using the ? operator as shown in Figure 4-5.

The ? operator in Figure 4-5 allows either statement to be executed based on the outcome of the test **guess>magic**. After being evaluated, the first or second expression becomes the value of the entire operation. Like all other C functions, **printf( )** may be used in expressions. The value of a function is determined by executing it and using its return value. In the case of Figure 4-5, the return value is not of interest, but in the process the appropriate string gets printed.

```
main()   /* magic number program */
{
     int magic = 123;   /* magic number */
     int guess;

     guess = getnum():   /* read an integer from the keyboard */
     if (guess == magic)
     {
          printf("** Right **");
          printf("%d is the magic number",magic);
     }        .
     else
          guess > magic ? printf("High") : printf("Low");
}
```

Figure 4-5. Magic Number Program using the ? operator

The *switch* Statement

Although the **if-else-if** ladder can perform a sequence of tests, it is hardly elegant. The code can be hard to follow and can confuse even the programmer at a later date. For these reasons, C has a built-in multiple-branch decision statement called **switch**. The **switch** statement acts somewhat like the **ON-GOTO** and **ON-GOSUB** in BASIC, testing a variable successively against a list of integer or character constants. When a match is found, a statement or block of statements is executed. The general form of the **switch** statement is

```
switch(variable) {
    case constant1:
        statement;
    case constant2:
        statement;
    case constant3:
        statement;
        .
        .
        .
    default:
        statement;
}
```

where **default** is performed if no matches are found. The **default** is optional, and if not present, no action takes place if all matches fail.

The **switch** differs from the **if** because **switch** can only test for equality, whereas the **if** can evaluate a relational or logical expression.

The **switch** statement is often used to process keyboard commands like the menu selection. As shown here with its BASIC equivalent, the function **menu( )** will display a menu for a spelling checker program and will call the proper procedures:

```
menu()
{
        char ch;

        printf("1. Check Spelling\n");
        printf("2. Correct Spelling errors\n");
        printf("3. Display Spelling Errors\n");
        printf("Strike Any Other Key to Skip\n");
        printf("       Enter your choice: ");
        ch=getchar();   /* read the selection from
                            the keyboard */
        switch(ch) {
                case '1':
                        check_spelling();
                        break;
                case '2':
                        correct_errors();
                        break;
                case '3':
                        display_errors();
                        break;
                default :
                        printf("No option selected");
        }
}

10 PRINT "1. Check Spelling"
20 PRINT "2. Correct Spelling Errors"
30 PRINT "3. Display Spelling Errors"
40 PRINT "Enter Any Other Number to Skip"
50 PRINT "       Enter your choice: ";
60 INPUT A
70 ON A GOSUB 100,200,300,400,400,400,400,400,400,400
80 END
100 REM CHECK SPELLING
120 RETURN
200 REM CORRECT ERRORS
210 RETURN
300 REM DISPLAY ERRORS
310 RETURN
400 PRINT "No option selected"
410 RETURN
```

The BASIC version differs slightly from the C version because the BASIC version uses **INPUT**, which will wait for a carriage return. (The BASIC version did not use the **INKEY$** command because older versions of BASIC do not support it.)

The **break** statement used inside each **case** of the **switch** causes the program flow to exit from the entire **switch** statement and continue on to the next statement outside the **switch**. If the **break** statements are not included, all of the statements *at and below the match will be executed.* You can think of a **case** as a label that signifies where execution should pick up after a selection is read from the keyboard. Unlike **break**, **case** does not stop execution. These aspects of the **switch** can be an advantage at times, as shown here:

```
func1()
{
        int ch, flag;
        ch=getnum();

        flag = -1;
        switch(ch) {
                case 1:
                case 2:
                case 3:
                        flag=0;
                        break;
                case 4:
                        flag=1;
                case 5:
                        error(flag);
                        break;
        }
}

10 INPUT C
20 F = -1
30 ON C GOTO 100, 200, 300, 400, 500
40 END
100 REM DROP THROUGH
200 REM DROP THROUGH
300 F = 0
310 GOTO 40
400 F = 1
500 GOSUB 1000
GOTO 40
1000 REM CALL AN ERROR ROUTINE
1010 RETURN
```

This routine illustrates two facets of the **switch** statement. First, you can have empty conditions. In this case, the first three constants will all execute the same statements:

```
flag=0;
break;
```

Second, execution will continue into the next **case** if a **break** statement is not present. If **ch** matches 4, **flag** is set to 1, and because there is no **break** statement, execution will continue and the statement **error(flag)** will be executed. In this case, **flag** will have the value 1. If **ch** had matched 5, then **error(flag)** would have been called with a **flag** value of −1.

Loops

In C and all other modern programming languages, *loops* allow a set of instructions to be performed until a certain condition is reached. This condition may be predefined, as in the **for** loop, or open-ended, as in the **while** and **do-while** loops.

The for Loop

The **for** loop is used when you want to execute statements more than once. Figure 4-6 compares a C program using **for** and a BASIC program using **FOR-NEXT**. Both programs will print the word **HELLO** and the value of **x**

```
10 FOR X=1 TO 100 STEP 1      main()
20    PRINT "HELLO ",X        {
30 NEXT                            int x;
                                   for(x=1;x<=100;++x)
                                        printf("HELLO %d",x);
                              }
```

Figure 4-6. A comparison of **for** in C and FOR-NEXT in BASIC

100 times on the screen. In the BASIC **FOR-NEXT** loop, lines 10 through 30 will be executed 100 times, each time increasing **x** by 1. In the C code, **x** is initially set to 1. Since **x** is less than 100, **printf( )** is called, **x** is increased by 1, and **x** is tested to see if it is still less than or equal to 100. This process repeats until **x** is greater than 100, when the calls to **printf( )** stop and the program terminates. In this example, **x** is the *loop control variable*, which is changed and checked each time the loop repeats.

The **FOR-NEXT** loop in BASIC and the **for** loop in C work in almost the same way: BASIC uses the keyword **NEXT** to define the end of the repeated code, while the iterative code in C is either the statement immediately following the **for** definition or a series of statements in a block.

The general form of **for** to repeat a single statement is

```
for(initialization; condition; increment)
    statement;
```

To repeat a block, the general form is

```
for(initialization; condition; increment)
{
    statement 1;
    .
    .
    .
    statement n;
}
```

The *initialization* is usually an assignment statement that is used to set the loop-control variable. The *condition* is a relational expression that determines when the loop will exit. The *increment* defines how the loop-control variable will change each time the loop is repeated. These three major sections must be separated by semicolons. The **for** loop will continue to execute as long as the condition tests true. Once the condition becomes false, program execution will resume on the statement following the **for** block.

This is an example of a **for** loop that contains multiple statements:

```
for(x=100;x!=65;x=x-5)
{
        z=sqrt(x);
        printf("The square root of %d, %f",x,z);
}
```

Both the **sqrt( )** call and the **printf( )** call will be executed until **x** equals 65.

Note that the loop is *negative running*: **x** was initialized to 100, and 5 is subtracted from it each time the loop repeats.

An important point about **for** loops in C is that the conditional test is always performed at the top of the loop. This means that the code inside the loop may not be executed at all if the condition is false to begin with. This loop, for example,

```
x=10;
for(y=10; y!=x; ++x)
{
        printf("%d",y);
}
printf("%d",y);
```

will never execute because **x** and **y** are in fact equal. After the loop, **y** will still have the value 10 assigned to it, and the only output will be the number 10 printed once.

A **for** loop in C has several capabilities with no parallel in BASIC. For example, multiple loop variables can be used and their conditions checked, as shown in this loop:

```
for(x=0,y=0;x+y<10;++x)
{
        y=getchar();
        y=y-'0';        /* subtract the ascii code for 0
                           from y */
}
```

Commas separate the two initialization statements. This is necessary in order for the compiler to understand that there are two initialization statements, not one initialization and a condition. Each time that **x** is incremented, the loop repeats and the value of **y** is set by keyboard input. Both **x** and **y** must be at the correct value for the loop to terminate. You must initialize **y** to 0 so that its value is defined. If **y** were not defined, it would be possible that **y** could, by chance or by earlier program usage, contain a 10, thereby making the conditional test false and preventing the loop from executing.

In general, the condition may be any relational or logical C statement. It is not limited only to testing the loop control variables, as you can see in this example:

```
sign_on()
{
        char str[20];   /* define a 20 char-string */
        int x;
```

```
for(x=0;x<3 && strcmp(str,"password");++x)
{
        printf("enter password please:");
        gets(str);
}
if(x==3) hang_up();
}
```

You can use the **sign—on( )** function as a security measure to allow only users who know the password access to a certain computer. If the user types the password correctly in the first three attempts, then **x** will be less than 3 because the conditional test becomes false. Otherwise, the loop terminates when **x** equals 3.

The function **strcmp( )** is a standard library function. It will compare two strings and return 0 if they match. Otherwise, it will return the character position where they first differed.

Another capability of **for** allows both the initialization and the incrementation portions to have multiple arguments. For example, this loop is perfectly valid:

```
for(x=0,y=100;x<y;++x,--y)
        printf("%d %d\n",x,y);
```

Remember that the three major portions of the loop—the initialization, the condition, and the increment—are separated by semicolons. Any additional arguments are separated by commas.

Another aspect of the **for** loop that is different in C is that pieces of the loop definition need not be there. If you wanted to write a loop that would run until a certain number was typed at the keyboard, it could look like this:

```
for(x=0;x!=123; )
{
    x=getnum( ); /* get a number from keyboard */
    .
    .
    .
}
```

The increment portion of the **for** definition is blank. This means that each time the loop repeats, **x** is tested to see if it equals 123, but no further action takes place. If, however, you type 123 at the keyboard, the loop condition is false and the loop exits. Unlike the BASIC **FOR-NEXT** loop, which assumes that the increment is 1 if the **step** command is missing, the C **for** loop will take no action if the increment section is missing.

Initialization can be moved outside the loop. For example,

```
x=0;
for( ;x<10; )
{
        printf("%d",x);
        ++x;
}
```

Here the initialization section has been left blank and **x** is initialized before the loop is entered.

Even more can be deleted from the loop definition. You can test for the condition inside the repeated code and terminate the loop using the **break** statement. The **break** essentially forces an exit from a loop. (**break** will be discussed later in this chapter.) Program control would then pick up at the code following the loop, as shown:

```
x=10;
for(;; )
{
        x=getchar();  /* get a character */
        if(x=='A') break;  /* exit the loop */
}
printf("you typed an A");
```

This loop will run until an **A** is typed at the keyboard.

Time delay loops are often used in C programs. This is an example of one in both C and BASIC:

```
for(x=0;x<1000;++x)  ;    10 FOR X=1 TO 1000
                          20 NEXT
```

Both pieces of code do the same thing: they increment **x** to 1000 but take no further action. The semicolon is necessary in the C version because the **for** expects a statement, which can be empty, or a block of statements.

The while Loop

Another form of a built-in loop is **while**. The general form of the statement is

while(condition) statement;

where *statement* may be a single statement or a block of statements that is to be repeated. The *condition* may be any expression, with true being any non-zero value. The statement is performed while the condition is true. When the condition becomes false, program control passes to the line after the loop code.

Many BASICs have a **WHILE-WEND** statement, which works in almost the same way as the **while** loop in C. The following example shows both the C and BASIC versions of a keyboard-input routine that simply loops until **A** is pressed.

```
wait_for_char()                          10 A$=""
{                                        20 WHILE A$<>"A"
        char ch;                         30     INPUT A$
                                         40 WEND
        ch=0;    /* initialize ch */
        while(ch!='A')  ch=getchar();
}
```

In the C version you can see that first **ch** is initialized to 0. As a local variable, its value is not known when **wait—for—char( )** is executed. The **while** loop then begins by checking if **ch** is not equal to **A**. Because **ch** was initialized to 0 beforehand, the test is true and the loop begins. Each time a key is pressed on the keyboard, the test is tried. Once an **A** is pressed, the condition becomes false because **ch** equals **A**, and the loop terminates.

Like the **for** loop, **while** loops check the condition at the top of the loop, which means that the loop code may not execute at all. This eliminates having to perform a test before the loop. A good illustration of this is the function **pad( )**, which will add spaces to the end of a string up to a predefined length. If the string is already that length, no spaces will be added.

```
pad(s,length)
char *s;
int length;
{
        int l;

        l=strlen(s);  /* find out how long it is */
        while(l<length) {
                s[l] = ' ';   /* insert a space */
                l++;
        }
        s[l]='\0';        /* strings need to be
                             terminated in a null */
}
```

In **pad( )**, the two arguments are s, the string, and **length**, the number of characters s will be lengthened to. In Chapter 3 you saw that when passing a string into a function, you can simply use its array name without any indexes. To receive the string (the character array), you must declare the formal parameter s to be of type **char pointer** using the line

```
char *s;
```

This allows you to access the string directly, element by element. (Passing strings to functions will be explained more completely in Chapter 5.)

If the string s is already equal to or greater than **length**, the code inside the **while** loop will never execute. If s is less than **length**, **pad( )** will add the required number of spaces onto the string. The **strlen( )** function, which you can find in the standard library, will return the length of the string.

Having several different statements inside a **while** that are each able to end the loop is a very common practice. A **while** loop may also have only a variable as the condition and may be used simply to repeat the set of instructions until the procedure is finished:

```
func1()
{
        int working;

        working=1;    /* i.e., true */
        while(working) {
                working=process1();
                if(working)
                        working=process2();
                if(working)
                        working=process3();
        }
}
```

Any of the three routines may return false (0) and cause the loop to exit.

There need not be any statements at all in the body of the **while** loop. For example,

```
while((ch=getchar()) != 'A') ;
```

will simply loop until **A** is typed at the keyboard. If you feel uncomfortable with the assignment inside the **while** condition, remember that the = sign is really just an operator in the sense that it returns a value: the value of the assignment operator is the value of the right-hand expression.

The do-while Loop

Unlike the **for** and **while** loops that test the loop condition at the top of the loop, the **do-while** loop checks its condition at the bottom of the loop. This means that a **do-while** loop will always execute at least once. The general form of the **do-while** loop is

```
do {
    statements;
} while(condition);
```

Although the braces are not necessary when only one statement is present, they are usually used to improve readability of the **do-while** construct.

There is no direct parallel in BASIC to the **do-while**, so when this type of loop is needed in a BASIC program, it must be constructed using **GOTO**s. Here are very simple examples of a **do-while** in C and a **GOTO** in BASIC:

```
do {                          10 INPUT N
        num=getnum();         20 IF N>100 THEN GOTO 10
} while(num>100);
```

Numbers will be read from the keyboard until a number is found that is less than 100.

Perhaps the most common use of the **do-while** is in a menu-selection routine in which the user makes a selection from a menu displayed on the screen. When a valid response is typed, it is returned as the value of the function. Invalid responses will cause the program to prompt again. The following is an improved version of **menu( )** from the spelling checker menu that was developed earlier in this chapter.

```
menu()
{
        char ch;

        printf("1. Check Spelling\n");
        printf("2. Correct Spelling Errors\n");
        printf("3. Display Spelling Errors\n");
        printf("Strike Any Other Key to Skip\n");
        printf("       Enter your choice: ");

        do {
            ch=getchar();        /* read the selection from
                                    the keyboard */
            switch(ch) {
                case '1':
                        check_spelling();
                        break;
                case '2':
                        correct_errors();
                        break;
                case '3':
                        display_errors();
                        break;
            }
        } while(ch!='1' && ch!='2' && ch!='3');
}
```

In the case of a menu function, you will always want it to execute at least once. After the options have been displayed, the program will loop until a valid option is selected.

Exiting Loops
Using *break* and *exit()*

The statement **break** and the library function **exit( )** allow you to force an exit from inside a loop, bypassing the normal loop condition.

The *break* Statement

When the **break** statement is encountered inside a loop, the loop is immediately terminated and program control resumes at the next statement following the loop. Figure 4-7 gives a simple example along with a BASIC comparison. Both versions will print the numbers 0 through 10 on the screen before ending. (Note that some versions of BASIC will not support a **GOTO** out of a **FOR** loop.)

The **break** statement is commonly used in loops in which a special condition can cause immediate termination. This is an example of such a situation, where a keypress can stop the execution of the program or routine:

```
look_up(name)
char *name;
{
        char tname[40];

        do {
                read_next_name(tname);
                if(key_press()) break;
        } while(!strcmp(tname,name));
}
```

You can use this function to find a name in a database file. If the file is very long and you are tired of waiting, you could strike a key and return from the function early. Both **read_next_name( )** and **key press( )** are user-defined functions.

The **strcmp( )** is a standard library function. It will compare two strings together and return 0 if they are equal. Otherwise it will return the character position where they first differed.

```
main()
{
        int t;
        for(t=0;t<100;t++0 {
                printf("%d ",t);
                if(t==10) break;
        }
}

10 FOR T=0 TO 99
20 PRINT T;
30 IF T=10 THEN GOTO 50
40 NEXT
50 END
```

Figure 4-7. The use of **break** in a C program and its BASIC equivalent

A **break** will cause an exit from only the innermost loop. For example,

```
for(t=0;t<100;+=t) {
        count=1;
        do {
                printf("%d ",count);
                count++;
                if(count==10) break;
        } while(1);  /* for ever */
}
```

will print the numbers 1 through 10 on the screen 100 times. Each time the **break** is encountered, control is passed back to the **for** loop.

A **break** used in a **switch** statement will affect only that **switch** and not any loop that the **switch** happens to be in.

The *exit( )* Function

A second way to terminate a loop from inside is by using the **exit( )** function, which is found in the standard library. Because the **exit( )** function will cause immediate termination of your program and return to the operating system, its use is somewhat limited. The **exit( )** function is traditionally called with an argument of 0 to indicate that termination is normal. Other arguments are used to indicate some sort of error. However, many micro-computer-based C compilers do not use the argument to **exit( )** in any way, so often you will see **exit( )** called with 0 as an argument under all circumstances.

A common use of **exit( )** occurs when a mandatory condition for the program's execution is not satisfied. For example, imagine a game in which a color graphics card must be present in the system. The **main( )** function might look like

```
main( )
{
    if(!color—card( )) exit(1);
    .
    .
    .
}
```

where **color—card( )** is a user-defined function that returns true if the color card is present. If the card is not in the system, **color—card( )** returns false and the program will terminate.

The **exit( )** function is also often associated with routines that open disk files. These types of routines will be discussed in Chapter 6.

The continue Statement

The **continue** statement works in almost the opposite way of the **break** statement: it forces the next iteration of the loop to take place, skipping any code in between. In BASIC, a **GOTO** would be used. For example,

```
do {                            10 INPUT X
        x=getnum();             20 IF X<0 GOTO 40
        if(x<0) continue;       30 PRINT X
        printf("%d ", x);       40 IF X<>100 GOTO 10
} while(x!=100);                50 END
```

Here only positive numbers are printed; a negative response will cause the loop to perform the termination test, **x!=100**, and start over again.

In **while** and **do-while** loops, a **continue** statement will cause control to go directly to the condition and then continue the looping process. In the case of the **for**, the increment part of the loop is performed, the condition is executed, and the loop continues. If you expanded the previous example so that it would only ask for a maximum of 100 numbers, it could be written like this:

```
for(t=0;t<100;++t) {
        x=getnum();
        if(x<0) continue;
        printf("%d ",x);
}
```

As you can see in the following example, **continue** can be used to expedite the exit from a loop by forcing the condition to be performed sooner.

```
code()
{
        char done, ch;

        done=0;
        while(!done) {
                ch=getchar();
                if(ch=='$') {
                        done=1;
                        continue;
                }
                putchar(ch+1);  /* shift the alphabet one
                                   position */
        }
}
```

You could use this function to code a message by shifting all characters one letter higher; for example, an "a" would become a "b." The function will terminate when a $ is pressed because the condition, brought into effect by **continue**, will find **done** to be true and will cause the loop to exit.

Labels and *goto*

This book will not make use of the **goto** outside of this section because in a language like C, which has a rich set of control structures and allows additional control using **break** and **continue**, there is little need for the **goto**. The chief concern most programmers have about the **goto** is its tendency to confuse a program and render it nearly unreadable. However, there are times when the use of the **goto** will actually clarify program flow rather than confuse it. If you will be using C as a replacement for assembler, you should at least be introduced to the **goto** because, under certain circumstances, it enables code to be very short and fast.

The **goto** requires a label for operation. A **label** may be any name that starts with a letter or an underscore followed by either letters, numbers, a single number, or the underscore character. The label name must be followed by a colon. For example, a loop from 1 to 100 could be written using **gotos** like this:

```
x=1;
loop1:
        x++;
        if(x<100) goto loop1;
```

A good use for the **goto** is as a way to exit from several layers of nesting. In this example

```
for(...) {
     for(...) {
          while(...) {
               if(...) goto stop;
               .
               .
               .
          }
     }
}
stop:
     printf("error in program \n");
```

eliminating the **goto** would cause a number of additional tests to be performed. A simple **break** statement would not work here because it would only exit from the innermost loop. If you substituted checks at each loop, the code would then look like this:

```
done=0
for(...) {
        for(...) {
                while(...) {
                        if(...) [
                                done=1;
                                break;
                        }
                        .
                        .
                        .
                {
                if(done) break;
                }
                if(done) break;
        }
}
```

You should use the **goto** sparingly, if at all. But if the code would be more difficult to read or if the execution speed of the code is critical, then by all means use the **goto**.

Putting the Pieces Together

Figure 4-8 gives the entire Magic Number Program. It uses much of what was described in this chapter, and you should make sure you understand all of the concepts used in the program before proceeding to the next chapter.

```
main()
{    /* magic number program */
     char option;
     int magic;
     do {
          printf("1. Define a new magic number\n");
          printf("2. Play\n");
          printf("3. Quit\n");
          do {
               printf("Enter your choice: ");
               option=getchar();
          } while(option<'1' || option >'3');
          switch(option) {
               case '1':
                    magic=next_magic();
                    break;
               case '2':
                    play(magic);
                    break;
               case '3':
                    printf("Goodbye\n");
                    break;
          }
     } while(option!='3');
}
next_magic()
{
     printf("enter new magic number: ");
     return (getnum());
}
getnum()
{
     char s[30];
     gets(s);
     return(atoi(s));
}
play(m)
int m;
{
     register int t;
     int x;
     for(t=0;t<100;t++) {
          printf("Guess the number: ");
          x=getnum();
          if(x==m) {
               printf("*** Right ***");
               return;
          }
          else
               if(x<m) printf("Too low\n");
               else printf("Too high\n");
     }
     printf("You used up all your guesses . . . try again\n");

     }
```

Figure 4-8. The complete Magic Number Program

E X E R C I S E S

1. Write a function called **max( )** that returns the value of the larger of its two integer arguments.

2. Write a function called **look—up( )** that has one character argument. If the argument is any of the following characters, return the characters indicated; otherwise, return the character "0." Hint: you should use the **switch** statement.

argument	return
1	a
2	b
3	c
4	d

3. Write the **look—up( )** function from the previous exercise using an **if-else-if** ladder.

4. Show three ways to write a function called **count( )** that simply print the numbers 1 to 100 on the screen. (Do not use the **goto**.)

5. Write a program that gets an integer from the keyboard, prints the message **hello** as many times as the number, and exits if the number is negative.

6. Compile and run the final Magic Number Program in Figure 4-8.

7. Improve the Magic Number Program so that it will tell the player how many guesses remain before the number of attempts runs out. Also create an integer array of ten elements, initialize the array with some integer values, and change **next—magic( )** to give the next element in the array.

A N S W E R S

1.
```
max(a,b)
{
        if(a>b) return(a);
        else return(b);
}
```

2.
```
look_up(c)
char c;
{
        switch(c) {
                case '1': return('a');
                case '2': return('b');
                case '3': return('c');
                case '4': return('d');
                default:  return('0');
        }
}
```

3.
```
look_up(c)
char c;
{
        if (c=='1') return('a');
        else if (c=='2') return('b');
        else if (c=='3') return('c');
        else if (c=='4') return('d');
        else return('0');
}
```

4.
```
count1()
{
        int t;

        for(t=0;t<100;++t) printf("%d",t);
}
```

```
        count2()
        {
                int t;

                t=0;
                while(t<100) printf("%d",t++);
        }

        count3()
        {
                int t;

                t=0;
                do {
                        printf("%d",t);
                        t++;
                } while(t<100);
        }
```

5. ```
   main()
   {
           int t;

           t=getnum();
           if(t<0) exit();
           for(;t>0;t--) printf("hello\n");
   }
   ```

7. ```
   int mcount;      /* this global will index into the magic
                       number array m[] */
   int m[10];       /* this array will hold the magic numbers */

   main()
   {       /* magic number program - improved */
           char option;
           int magic;

           init_magic();
           do {
                   printf("1. Define a new magic number\n");
                   printf("2. Play\n");
                   printf("3. Quit\n");
                   do {
                           printf("Enter your choice: ");
                           option=getchar();
                   } while(option<'1' || option >'3');
   ```

```
                  switch(option) {
                          case '1':
                                  magic=next_magic();
                                  break;
                          case '2':
                                  play(magic);
                                  break;
                          case '3':
                                  printf("Goodbye\n");
                                  break;
                  }
          } while(option!='3');
}

next_magic()
{
        mcount++;
        if(mcount>9) mcount=0; /* start over */
        return(m[mcount]);
}

getnum()
{
        char s[30];

        gets(s);
        return(atoi(s));
}

play(m)
int m;
{
        register int t;
        int x;
        for(t=0;t<100;t++) {
                printf("Guess the number: ");
                x=getnum();
                if(x==m) {
                        printf("*** Right ***");
                        return;
                }
                else
                        if(x<m) printf("Too low\n");
                        else printf("Too high\n");
                printf("You have %d guesses remaining\n",99-t);
        }
        printf("You used up all your guesses . . . try again\n");
}

init_magic()
{
```

```
        mcount=0;
        m[0]=123;
        m[1]=23546;
        m[2]=245;
        m[3]=4634;
        m[4]=345;
        m[5]=7865;
        m[6]=341;
        m[7]=17956;
        m[8]=19;
        m[9]=2032;
}
```

Functions
In Detail
CHAPTER 5

Functions are C's building blocks in which all program activity occurs. Once a function has been written and debugged, it can be used again and again. This is one of the most important aspects of C as a programming language. This chapter discusses several aspects of writing and using functions in C. However, unlike earlier chapters, no parallel examples in BASIC will be given because C functions and BASIC functions are so dissimilar.

The Form
Of a Function

As you will recall from Chapter 1, the general form of a C function is

```
function_name(parameter list)
parameter declarations;
{
    body of the function;
}
```

The number of parameters may be zero. If there are no parameters, you don't need a declaration portion.

Return Values

All functions return a value. This value can be either explicitly specified by the **return** statement, or it can be 0 if no other value is specified. Functions will return integer values by default. Other types of values may be returned if specified, as will be discussed later in this chapter.

A function may be used in expressions because each function has a value that is either a returned value or 0 by default. Therefore, each of the following expressions is valid in C:

```
x=power(y);
if(max(x,y) > 100) printf("greater");
for(ch=getchar();isdigit(ch);) ... ;
```

However, a function cannot be the target of an assignment; a statement such as

```
swap(x,y)=100  /* incorrect statement */
```

is wrong. Your compiler will flag it as an error and not compile your program.

Although all functions in C have return values, when you write programs, your functions will generally be of three types. The first type of function is specifically designed to perform operations on its arguments and return a value based on that operation. Examples of this sort of function are **sqrt( )** and **max( )**.

The second type of function manipulates information and returns a value that simply indicates the success or failure of that manipulation. An example is **write( )**, which is used to write information to a disk file. If the write operation is successful, **write( )** returns a "true" value; if it is unsuccessful, it returns a "false" value.

The last type of function will have no explicit return value. In essence, the function is merely a procedure that produces no value. An example is **sort( )**, a function that will sort data. Because all data can be sorted, a return value is not meaningful since it will always be true. (However, if you had written a sort function that operated on only one class of data, an error

```
main()
{
    int x,y,z;
    x=10;    y=20;
    z=mul(x,y);                /* 1 */
    printf("%d",mul(x,y));     /* 2 */
    mul (x,y);                 /* 3 */
}
```

Figure 5-1. A program showing the use of return functions

return code that indicated incorrect input would be meaningful.) Therefore, although all functions return values, you don't necessarily have to use them for anything.

A very common question concerning function return values is, Don't I have to assign this value to some variable since a value is being returned? The answer is no. If there is no assignment specified, the value is simply discarded. For example, in line 1 of the program in Figure 5-1, the return value of **mul( )** is assigned to **z**. In line 2, the return value is not actually assigned, but is used by the **printf( )** function. Finally, in line 3, the return value is lost because it is neither assigned to another variable nor used as part of an expression.

The Scope of Variables

You learned in Chapter 3 about the scope and lifetime of variables. A local variable is *dynamic*; it is created when the function is executed and destroyed when the function is finished. In other words, a local variable is known only to the function in which it is declared.

A global variable is declared outside of any function and is known to all functions in the program. Global variables stay in existence throughout the entire duration of the program.

A **static** variable will hold its value inside a function from call to call. It is known only to its function or file and will stay in existence during the program.

Function Arguments

Function arguments have been used so far with little explanation because, for the most part, function argument usage is intuitive. You will seldom have to think about it when writing functions. However, as a C programmer, you must understand how C passes arguments to functions so that you can control how data is manipulated by using some of C's most advanced and efficient features.

Call by Value
And Call by Reference

Arguments can generally be passed to functions in one of two ways. The first is called *call by value*. This method copies the *value* of each of the arguments into the formal parameters of the function. With this method changes made to the parameters of the function have no effect on the variables used to call the function.

Call by reference is the second way a function can have arguments passed to it. In this method, the *address* of each argument is copied into the parameters of the function. This means that changes made to the parameter will affect the variable used to call the function.

C functions use call by value. This means, in general, that you cannot alter the variables used to call the function. (You will learn later in this chapter how to "force" a call by reference to allow changes to the calling variables.) For example, in the following function:

```
sqr(x)
int x;
{
        x=x*x;
        return(x);
}
```

if the argument to **sqr( )** is a constant, such as 10, the value 10 is copied into the parameter **x**. When the assignment **x=x∗x** takes place, the only thing modified is the local variable **x**. The constant 10 is not affected.

The same process takes place when **sqr( )** is called with a variable. For example, if **y** equals 100, the call **sqr(y)** will result in the value of variable **y** being copied into the parameter **x**. Under no circumstance is **y** itself modified.

Remember that a copy of the value of the variable or constant used to call a function is passed into that function. What occurs inside the function will have no effect on the variable used in the call.

Since all C arguments are passed by value, changing the variables used in the call is not possible. However, C does allow you to simulate a call by reference by using pointers to pass the address of a variable into a function and to change the variable used in the call. As you will recall from Chapter 3, pointers are simply the addresses of variables. You can pass an address into a function just like any other value. The function **swap( )**, which exchanges the value of its two integer arguments, is written as

```
swap(x,y)
int *x,*y;
{
        int temp;
        temp=*x;        /* get the value at
                           address x */
        *x=*y;          /* put y into x */
        *y=temp;
}
```

But this is only half the story. After you have written the function **swap( )** you must use *addresses of the variables you wish to swap as the arguments when you call the function*. The program in Figure 5-2 shows the correct way to call **swap( )**.

The program in Figure 5-2 assigns the value 10 to the variable **x** and the value 20 to the variable **y**. Then **swap( )** is called, and the unary operator **&** is used to produce the addresses of the variables **x** and **y**. Therefore, the addresses of **x** and **y**, not their values, are passed into the function **swap( )**.

```
main()
{
    int x,y;
    x=10;
    y=20;
    swap(&x,&y);
}
```

Figure 5-2. A program showing the correct way to call **swap( )**

Inside **swap( )**, the unary operator * is used to indicate the value of the location pointed to by the address. In the statement **temp=*x**, the * operator produces the value pointed to by the address in **x** and assigns **temp** that value. In the statement ***x=*y**, the * operator "directs" the value at location **y** to be placed into the location found in **x**. The location **y** is then assigned the value of location **x**.

Chapter 7 is devoted to pointers because they are very important in C. However, the basic concepts were covered here since so many functions must be able to change the value of the variables used as arguments.

Before a function receives a pointer, you must define the type of data that it will be pointing to or else you may have some bizarre and unexpected results. Although integers and characters can usually be mixed freely in C, they cannot be when using pointers.

Calling Functions With Arrays

As you learned in Chapter 2, you can simply use the name of the character array without any index if you wish to call a function with a string argument. The same is true of all arrays passed as arguments to functions. However, C does not copy the entire array into the function. When you call a function with an array name, the address of the first element in the array is passed into the function. This means that the parameter declaration must be a pointer. For example, if you wished to write a program that input 10 numbers from the keyboard and printed them, you could write a program similar to the one in Figure 5-3.

In the **display( )** function shown in Figure 5-3, even though the argument is declared as an integer pointer, once inside the function, the entire array can be accessed using the normal array indexing. The reason for this is that arrays in C are really pointers to a region of memory, and in essence, the [ ] pair is an operator that finds the value of the data at that array index specified between the brackets. Because C has no bounds checking on arrays, the function also does not care how long the array is (but you must).

An array element used as an argument is treated like any other simple variable. For example, the program in Figure 5-3 could have been written without passing the entire array, as shown in Figure 5-4. The parameter to **display( )** is an integer. It is not relevant that **display( )** is called using an integer array element, because only that one value of the array is used.

However, when you use an array name as a function argument, it is

```
main()      /* print number */
{
      int t[10],i;

      for(i=0;i<10;++i) t[i]=getnum();
      display(t);
}
display(num)
int *num;
{
      int i;

      for(i=0;i<10;i++) printf("%d ",num[i]);
}
```

Figure 5-3.   A program that inputs and prints 10 numbers

passed by reference. You will be operating on and potentially altering the actual contents of the array elements used to call the function. For example, the program in Figure 5-5 prints a string as uppercase. The function **toupper( )**, found in most C libraries, will convert a lowercase character into an uppercase character. After the call to **print_upper( )**, the contents of array **s** in **main( )** will be changed to uppercase.

```
main()
{
      int t[10],i;

      for(i=0;i<10;++i) t[i]=getnum();
      for(i=0;i<10;i++) display(t[i]);
}
display(num)
int num;
{
      printf("%d ",num);
}
```

Figure 5-4.   A new version of the program in Figure 5-3 using an array element as an argument

```
    main()    /* print string as uppercase */
    {
                char s[80];
                gets(s);
                print_upper(s);
    }
    print_upper(string)
    char *string;
    {
                register int t;

                for(t=0;string[t];++t)   {
                        string[t]=toupper(string[t]);
                        putchar(string[t]);
                }
    }
```

Figure 5-5. A program that prints a string as uppercase

If you do not intend to change array s permanently, you could rewrite the same program as shown in Figure 5-6. In this version, the contents of array s remain unchanged because only its values—not the address—are passed into the function **print＿upper＿ch( )**.

```
    main()    /* print string as uppercase */
    {
            char s[80];
            int t;

            gets(s);
            for(t=0;s[t];++t) print_upper_ch(s[t]);
    }
    print_upper(ch)
    char *ch;
    {
            register int t;
            ch=toupper(ch);
                    putchar(ch);
    }
```

Figure 5-6. A new version of the program in Figure 5-5

A classic example of passing arrays into functions is found in the standard function **gets( )**, which you have already used in some examples. After being called with a single character array argument, **gets( )** will return a string that is typed at the keyboard. Although the **gets( )** in your standard library is much more sophisticated and complex, the function shown in the next listing will give you an idea of how it works. To avoid confusion with the standard function, this one is called **xgets( )**:

```
xgets(s)    /* very simple version of the standard gets()
            library function */
char *s;
{
        char ch;
        int t;

        for(t=0;t<80;++t) {
                ch=getchar();
                switch(ch) {
                        case '\n';
                                s[t]='\0'; /* terminate the string */
                                return;
                        case '\b':
                                if(t>0) t--;
                                break;
                        default:
                                s[t]=ch;
                                break;
                }
        }
        s[80]='0';
}
```

The **xgets( )** function must be called with a character pointer, which can be either a variable that you declared to be a character pointer, or the name of a character array, which by definition is a character pointer. Upon entry, **xgets( )** establishes a **for** loop from 0 to 80. This prevents very large strings from being entered at the keyboard. (Most standard library **gets( )** functions will not have a limit; it is included in this one to illustrate manual bounds checking to prevent array overruns.) If more than 80 characters are typed, the function will return. Because C has no built-in bounds checking, you should make sure that any variable used to call **xgets( )** can accept at least 80 characters. As you type characters on the keyboard, they are entered in the string. If you type a backspace, the counter **t** is reduced by 1. When you strike a carriage return, a null is placed at the end of the string, signaling its termination. Because the actual array used to call **xgets( )** is modified, upon return it will contain the characters that were typed in.

You could not write either **swap( )** or **xgets( )** without using pointers to create a call by reference. When writing such a function, remember that you must pass the *address* of the variable that you will be changing into the function. Inside the function, you must perform all operations on the variable by using the * unary operator.

The unary operator * can be thought of as "at address." For example, in

```
x=&z;
*x=10;
y=*x;
```

the first assignment statement, **x=&z;**, can be read as "assign **x** the address of **z**." The second assignment statement, ***x=10;**, can be read as "at address **x**, put the value 10." The final statement, **y=*x;**, can be read as "y equals the value at address **x**."

Remember the unary **&** as "the address of" and the ***** as "at address." If you can remember what the operators do, you will have fewer problems using them.

The Arguments argc and argv

Sometimes you need to pass information into a program when you run it. The general method is to pass information into the **main( )** function through the use of two special, built-in arguments: **argv** and **argc**. These are the only arguments that **main( )** can have. Figure 5-7 lists a short program that will print your name on the screen if you type it directly after the program name. If your name were Tom and you called this program "name," you would type **name Tom** to run the program. The output from the program would be **Hello Tom**. For example, if you were logged into drive A and were running MS-DOS, you would see

```
A>name Tom
Hello Tom
A>
```

after running the program **name**.

```
main(argc,argv) /* name program */
int argc;
char *argv[];
{
     if(argc!=2) {
               printf("You forgot to type your name\n");
               exit(0);
     }
     printf("Hello %s", argv[1]);
}
```

Figure 5-7. A program that prints the user's name on screen

Notice in Figure 5-7 that **main( )** has the two arguments **argv** and **argc**. Until now, there have not been any arguments to **main( )**. The arguments **argc** and **argv** are two built-in variables that allow you to use command-line arguments. A *command-line argument* is the information that follows the program's name on the command line of the operating system. For example, when you compile C programs, you type in something like

```
>cc program_name
```

after the prompt, where **program_name** is the program you wish compiled. The name of the program is passed into the C compiler as an argument to the program.

You can write your programs to take advantage of command-line arguments by using **argc** and **argv**. An **argc** contains the number of individual command-line strings. Each string is separated by a space. For example,

```
run Spot, run
```

is made up of three strings, while

```
Herb,Rick,Fred
```

is one single string. An **argc** will always be at least 1 because the name of the program that you are executing counts as the first argument.

An **argv** is a pointer to an array of strings. You must declare **argv** exactly as

```
char *argv[];
```

The empty brackets indicate that it is an array of undetermined length. You can now access the individual arguments by indexing **argv**. For example, **argv[0]** will point to the first string, which is always the program's name; **argv[1]** will point to the first argument, and so on.

A short example of using command-line arguments is the program called **countdown** shown in Figure 5-8. It will count down from some value and beep when it reaches 0. The length of the count is specified by the first command-line argument, which is assumed to be a number. The string containing the number is converted into an integer using the standard function **atoi( )** (ascii to integer), which is found in the C library, before the program will proceed. If the string **display** is present as the second command-line argument, the count will also be displayed on the screen. In **countdown**, if no arguments have been specified, the error message will be printed and execution stopped.

If you wish to access an individual element in one of the command strings, you may do so by adding a second index reference to **argv**. For example, the

```
main(argc, argv)           /* countdown */
int argc;
char *argv[];
{
    int disp, count;
    if(argc<2) {
        printf("you must enter the length of the count\n");
        printf("on the command line. Try again.\n");
        exit(0);
    }
    if(argc==3 && !strcmp(argv[2],"display"))
        disp=1;
    else disp=0;
    for(count=atoi(argv[1]);count;--count) {
        if(disp)  printf("%d ",count);
    }
    putchar(7);      /* this will ring the bell on most computers */
}
```

Figure 5-8. A program that uses command-line arguments

```
main(argc,argv)
int argc;
char *argv[];
{
        int t;

        for(t=0;t<argc;++t)  {
                i=0;

                while(argv[t][i])  {
                        putchar(argv[t][i]);
                        ++i;
                }
        }
}
```

Figure 5-9. A program that prints all of the arguments used to call it

program in Figure 5-9 will display all the arguments with which it was called and display them on the screen a character at a time.

The double brackets in **putchar(argv[t][i]);** of Figure 5-9 may look funny to you, but they are perfectly valid. The first index accesses the string and the second index accesses the character of that string. You will learn more about this type of indexing in the chapter on arrays.

Usually you will use **argc** and **argv** to get initial commands into your program. In theory, you can have 32,767 arguments, but most operating systems will not allow more than a few. You normally use these arguments to indicate a file name or an option. Using command-line arguments will give your program a very professional appearance and facilitate the program's use in batch files.

Functions Returning
Non-Integer Values

All examples of functions so far have returned either integer values or character values, which are automatically converted to integers. The integer value is the default data type that C functions return when no other is specified. You will find that the vast majority of your functions will use this default. However, there will be times when you will find it necessary to return another type of data.

Functions may be declared to return any of the built-in data types found in C. The method of declaration is similar to that of variables: the same type specifiers are used and the type specifier precedes the function name. The general form of declaration is

type—specifier function—name(parameter list)
    parameter declarations;
    {
        body of function statements;
    }

The type specifier does not have to go on the same line as the function name; for example,

```
float
fsum(x,y)
float x,y;
{
    return(x+y);
}
```

The type specifier tells the compiler what type of data the function is to return. This information is critical if the program is going to run correctly, because different data types have different sizes and internal representations. An integer may be 2 bytes long, whereas a floating point number might be 8 bytes in length. For example, if your function returned a **float** and the calling function thought it was an integer, only the first two bytes of the **float** would be used. This, of course, would be useless.

There is a second thing you must do when using a return value other than an integer. Your calling routine must know the type of data that the function is actually returning, so you must declare the function inside the calling routine. For example, Figure 5-10 shows how to use the floating-point function **sum( )** inside a program. The declaration line not only declares the variables **first** and **second,** but the function **sum( )** as well. This only tells the compiler that **sum( )** will return a floating-point data type. It does not declare a variable with the name **sum** and it does not affect what type of data **sum( )** actually returns.

If you have a mismatch between the type of data that the function returns and the type of data that the calling routine expects, you will have bizarre

```
        main()
        {
                float first, second, sum();
                first=123.23;
                second=99.09;
                printf("%f",sum(first,second));
        }

        float sum(a,b)
        float a,b;
        {
                return a+b;
        }
```

Figure 5-10.   A program using **sum( )**

and unpredictable results. If both functions are in the same file, the compiler will catch the type mismatch. However, if they are in different files, the compiler will not find the error. Type checking is not done at link time or run time, but only at compile time. Therefore, you must be very careful to make sure that both types are compatible.

As mentioned earlier, when a character is returned from a function declared to be of type integer, the character value is converted into an integer. Because C can handle the conversion from character to integer and back again, functions returning character values will often use the default type conversion into integers and not specifically declare a function that returns a character type.

Returning Pointers

Although functions that return pointers are handled exactly the same as any other type of function, a few important concepts will be discussed.

Pointers to variables are *neither* integers *nor* unsigned integers. They are pointers. The reason for this distinction lies in the fact that pointers may be incremented and decremented. Each time a pointer is incremented, for example, the pointer will point to the next data item of its type. Since each data type may be of different length, C must know what type of data the pointer is pointing to in order to make it point to the next data item. Pointer arithmetic will be explained in Chapter 7, but it is critical that you do not try to use integers to return addresses of variables.

If you wanted to write a function that would return a pointer into a string at the place where a character match was found, you could use this:

```
char *match(c,s);
char c, *s;
{
    int count;
    count==0;
    while(c!=s[count] && s[count]!='\0') count++;
    return(&s[count]);
}
```

The function **match( )** will attempt to return a pointer to the place in a string where the first match was found with the character in **c**. If no match is found, a pointer to the null terminator will be returned.

Figure 5-11 gives a short program that uses **match( )**. This program reads a string and then a character. If the character is in the string, the program prints the string from the point of match. Otherwise, it prints the message **no match found**.

```
main()
{
    char s[80], *p;
    gets(s);
    ch=getchar();
    p=match(ch,s);
    if(p!=0)   /* there is a match */
            printf("% ", p);
    else
            printf("no match found");
}
```

Figure 5-11. A program using **match( )**

Recursion

In C, functions may call themselves. A function is *recursive* if a statement in the body of the function calls itself. Sometimes called *circular definition*, recursion is the process of defining something in terms of itself. Standard BASICs do not allow recursion.

There are many examples of recursion. A recursive way to define an integer number is as the digits 0, 1, 2, 3, 4, 5, 6, 7, 8, 9, plus or minus an integer number. For example, the number 15 is the number 7 plus the number 8; 21 is 9 plus 12; and 12 is 9 plus 3.

For a computer language to be recursive, a function must be able to call itself. A simple example is the function **factr( )**, which computes the factorial of an integer. The factorial of a number is the product of all the integers between 1 and that number. For example, 3 factorial is $1 \times 2 \times 3$, or 6. Here is a nonrecursive version called **fact( )**:

```
fact(n)           /* non-recursive */
int n;
{
    int t,answer;
    answer=1;
    for(t=1;t<n;t++)
            answer=answer*(t);
    return(answer);
}
```

This is the recursive version **factr( )**:

```
factr(n)          /* recursive */
int n;
{
    int answer;
    if(n==1) return(1);
    answer=factr(n-1)*n;
    return(answer);
}
```

The nonrecursive version of **fact( )** should be clear: it uses a loop starting at 1 and ending at the number n and progressively multiples each number by the moving product.

When the recursive **factr( )** is called with an argument of 1, the function returns 1; otherwise it returns the product of **factr(n−1)*n**. To evaluate this expression, **factr( )** is called with **n−1**. This happens until **n** equals 1 and the functions begin returning.

If you wanted to compute the factorial of 2, the first call to **factr( )** will cause a second call to be made with the argument of 1. This call will return 1, which is then multiplied by 2 (the original **n** value). The answer is then 2. In one of the exercises at the end of this chapter, you will put print statements into **factr( )**, which will show at what level each call is and what the intermediate answers are.

When a function calls itself, new local variables and parameters are allocated storage on the stack, and the function code is executed with these new variables from the start. A recursive call does not make a new copy of the function. Only the arguments are new. As each recursive call returns, the old local variables and parameters are removed from the stack, and execution resumes at the point of the function call inside the function. Recursive functions could be said to "telescope" out and back.

Most recursive routines do not significantly save code size or variable storage. The recursive versions of most routines may execute a bit more slowly because of the added function calls, but this will not be noticeable in most cases. Many recursive calls to a function could cause a stack overrun, but this is unlikely. Because storage for function parameters and local variables is on the stack, and because each new call creates a new copy of these variables, it is possible that the stack could "walk on" some other data or program memory. However, you probably will not have to worry about this unless a recursive function runs wild.

A recursive function can sometimes be clearer and simpler to write than the same iterative one. Some people seem to think recursively more easily than others. If you feel comfortable with recursion, then use it. If you do not, use iterative methods. Very few examples in this book will be recursive, and when one is, the reason will be pointed out.

When writing recursive functions, you must have an **if** statement somewhere to force the function to return without the recursive call being executed. If you don't do this and you call the function, it will never return. This is a very common error when writing recursive functions. Use **printf( )** and **getchar( )** liberally during development so you can watch what is going on and abort execution if you see that you have made a mistake.

Writing Your Own Functions

You have already been writing some functions, but parameters and efficiency are worth covering now.

Parameters and General-Purpose Functions

You should not base general-purpose functions on global data. All of the information that a function needs should be passed to it by its parameters. In the few cases that this is not possible, you should use **static** variables.

Besides making your functions general-purpose, you should use parameters in place of global variables to keep your code readable and less susceptible to bugs that result from side effects.

Efficiency

The use of functions greatly improves the readability and efficiency of most programs and helps prevent errors due to side effects. However, in certain specialized applications, you may need to place the code "in line" instead of into a function. The *only* time you should restrict your use of function calls is when execution time is critical.

There are two reasons that line code is faster than a function call. First, a call instruction takes time to execute. Second, if there are arguments to pass, they have to be placed on the stack, which also takes time. For almost all applications, this very slight increase in execution time is of no significance. But if execution time is important, remember that each function call uses time that would be saved if the code in the function were placed in line. For example, Figure 5-12 gives two versions of a program that prints the square of the numbers from 1 to 10. The in-line version will run faster than the other because the function call takes time.

```
in line                          function call
main()                           main()
{                                {
      int x;                           int x;

      for(x=1;x<11;++x)                for(x=1;x<11;++x)
            printf("%d",x*x);                printf("%d",sqr(x));
}                                }

                                 sqr(a)
                                 int a;
                                 {
                                       return a*a;
                                 }
```

Figure 5-12. The in-line and function-call versions of a program that prints the square of the numbers from 1 to 10

Files and Libraries

After you have written a function, you can do three things with it: you can just leave it in the same file as the **main( )** function, you can put it in a separate file with other functions that you have written, or you can place it into a library.

Judging a Program File's Size

When you first start writing C programs, the tendency is to leave all of your functions in the same file as **main( )**. This is acceptable in the beginning because your early programs tend to be rather short. However, when you start developing larger programs, you will run into a couple of problems.

First, compilation time is directly related to the size of the program that is being compiled. A good aspect of C is that once you have debugged a function, you can put it into a separate file and simply link it in. The linking process is much shorter than compiling, and it eliminates the need to recompile working code constantly.

Second, large files tend to be difficult to edit, especially in a program-development and debugging cycle. This can waste valuable time and add to your frustration.

For most microcomputers, a source file that is longer than 10,000 bytes should be broken into pieces and compiled separately. Most programmers prefer to work with files of less than 5000 bytes.

Separate Files

Before you begin to break your functions into separately compiled files, it is important that you plan ahead. One of the most frustrating yet common tasks you will have to do while working on a large program is search each file to try to find where you put a certain function. A little organization early on will help avoid this problem.

First, group all functions that are conceptually related together into a file. For example, if you are writing a text editor, you can put all functions that are required to delete text in one file, all those that search text in another, and so on.

Second, put all general-purpose functions for your program together. For example, in database programs the input/output formatting functions belong in a separate file because they will be used by various other functions.

Third, group top-level functions in either a separate file or, if there is room, in the **main( )** file. Top-level functions are used to initiate the general activity of the program. These routines essentially define the operation of the program.

Some organizing of your functions files is important because you will need to find a specific function later. There are many ways to organize them and you should find the organization best suited to your style of programming.

Libraries

A library of functions differs from a separately compiled file of functions. In a library, only the functions that your program actually uses are loaded and linked together with your program. In a separately compiled file, *all* of the functions in that file are loaded and linked together with your program. For most of the function files that you will create, you will probably want all of the functions in the file anyway. In the case of the C standard library, you would never want *all* of the functions linked into your program because this would make your object code huge.

There may be times when you would like to create a library. For example, suppose you had written a very special set of statistical functions. You would not want all of these functions loaded in if your program only needed to find the mean of some set of values. In this case, a library would be useful.

Most C compilers will include instructions on creating a library. Since the process varies from compiler to compiler, you should study your user manual to find out what procedure you should follow.

EXERCISES

1. Write a function called **pr_rev( )** that reads a string input from the keyboard and prints it in reverse. For example, **hello** would be printed **olleh**.

2. Find what is wrong with the following function and try to fix it:

```
next_record()   /* returns the next record in a file */
{
     int next;
     next++;
     seek(next);
     read record();
}
```

3. Write a function called **power( )** that will accept two integer arguments. The first argument is the base and the second is the exponent. Write **power( )** so that the first argument contains the answer after the function returns. Use the return value of the function to indicate math overflow; that is, return a 1 if the operation was a success or a 0 if

an overflow occurred. Assume both arguments are positive. Hint: if math overflow occurs, the number will become negative.

4. Modify the program **countdown** in Figure 5-8 to allow the arguments **count** and **display** to be in any order. For example,

```
countdown 1000 display
```

is the same as

```
countdown display 1000
```

5. Write two functions, **code( )** and **decode( )**, that accept a string for an argument. The **code( )** function should modify the argument string by adding 1 to all characters in it except the null terminator. The **decode( )** function restores the coded string to its original form.

6. Using the functions **code( )** and **decode( )** from the previous exercise, write a short program that will accept a string on the command line, print the string coded, and then print it decoded. If no string is specified on the command line, prompt for one.

7. Write a recursive function called **print_num( )** that has one integer argument. It will print the numbers from 1 to **n** on the screen, where **n** is the value of the argument.

ANSWERS

```
1. pr rev()
   {
            int t;
            char s[80];

            gets(s);
            for(t=strlen(s);t;t--) putchar(s[t-1]);
   }
```

2. The local variable **next** is dynamic and will not maintain a value between function calls. The solution is to make **next** a **static** variable.

```
3. power(x,y)
   int *x,*y;
   {
        int temp;
        temp=*x;
        if(*y==0) {
             *x=1;   /* anything to power of 0 is 1 */
             return 1;
        }
        (*y)--;
        for(;*y;(*y)--) {
             *x=(*x) * temp;
             if(*x<0) return 0;
        }
        return 1;
   }
```

```
4. main(argc,argv)              /* count down */
   int argc;
   char *argv[];
   {
      int disp, count;
      char d[80],c[80];
      if(argc<2) {
           printf("you must enter the length of the count\n");
           printf("on the command line. Try again.\n");

           exit(0);
      }
```

```
    if(argc==3) {
        if(!strcmp(argv[1],"display")) {
            strcpy(d,argv[1]);
            strcpy(c,argv[2]);
        }
        else {
            strcpy(d,argv[2]);
            strcpy(c,argv[1]);
        }
    }
    if(argc==3 && !strcmp(d,"display"))
        disp=1;
    else disp=0;
    for(count=atoi(c);count;--count) {
        if(disp)  printf(" ",count);
    }
    putchar(7);      /* this will ring the bell on most
                        computers */
}
```

5.
```
code(s)
char *s;
{
    register int t;
    for(t=0;s[t];++t) s[t]=s[t]+1;
}
decode(s)
char *s;
{
    register int t;
    for(t=0;s[t];++t) s[t]=s[t]-1;
}
```

6.
```
main(argc,argv)
int argc;
char *argv[];
{
    char s[80];
    if(argc!=2) {
        printf("enter your message: ");
        gets(s);
    }
    else strcpy(s,argv[1]);
    code(s);
    printf(s);
    printf('\n");
    decode(s);
    printf(s);
}
```

```
code(s)
char *s;
{
     register int t;
     for(t=0;s[t];++t) s[t]=s[t]+1;
}
decode(s)
char *s;
{
     register int t;
     for(t=0;s[t];++t) s[t]=s[t]-1;
}
```

7. ```
   print num(n)
   int n;
   {
        if(n==1) printf("%d ",n);
        else {
             print num(n-1);
             printf("%d ",n);
        }
   }
   ```
   ```

Input, Output, And Disk Files

CHAPTER 6

This chapter discusses how to read and write from the console and disk files. You will learn about the many standard C library functions that are designed to help you do this.

Remember that there are no built-in functions to perform I/O operations in C. Instead, all of these functions are found in the C standard library. In previous chapters, you have already used the functions **printf( )**, **getchar( )**, and **gets( )**, which are just a few of the functions available to you.

In C all I/O is *character-oriented*. This not only includes reading and writing to the console (that is, the keyboard and screen), but to the disk file functions as well. This differs from BASIC, in which you can read and write strings and numbers directly. In C you read and write bytes. As you have seen in the functions **gets( )** and **getnum( )**, it is possible to write functions that read strings and numbers, but these functions still use calls to the character-oriented I/O functions.

Console I/O

Console I/O refers to operations that occur at the keyboard and screen of your computer. While you have already used some of these functions, this section will discuss and clarify some important aspects of their usage.

If you only know I/O in BASIC, be warned that the I/O in C is completely different. In BASIC, all console I/O is performed using high-level built-in functions. Although some BASICs do support the **INKEY$** for returning one character, it is not the primary form of console input.

The *getchar( )* and *putchar( )* Functions

The simplest of the console I/O functions are **getchar( )**, which reads a character from the standard input (usually the keyboard), and **putchar( )**, which prints a character to the standard output (usually the screen).

The **getchar( )** function waits until a key is pressed and then returns its value. Generally, **getchar( )** will also "echo" the character you type to the screen automatically. This means that the character you type at the keyboard will be explicitly written to the screen in order to be displayed without being echoed. It will not automatically appear because there is no connection between the keyboard and the screen.

The **putchar( )** function will write its character argument to the screen of your computer only if that argument is part of the character set that your computer can display.

The program in Figure 6-1 will input characters from the keyboard and print them in reverse case: uppercase will print as lowercase, and lowercase as uppercase. The program halts when a period is typed.

The function **islower( )** will return true if **ch** is a lowercase character. The function **toupper( )** will convert a lowercase letter into an uppercase letter and **tolower( )** will convert an uppercase letter into a lowercase one. These functions will not affect nonalphabetic characters like + or ?. These functions are found in the standard library.

The *gets( )* and *puts( )* Functions

On the next step, in terms of complexity and power, are the functions **gets( )** and **puts( )**. They enable you to read and write strings of characters at the console.

```
main()   /* case switcher */
{
        char ch;
        do {
                ch=getchar();
                if(islower(ch)) putchar(toupper(ch));
                else putchar(tolower(ch));
        } while (ch!='.'); /* use a period to stop*/
}
```

Figure 6-1. A program that inputs characters and prints them in reverse case

The **gets( )** function returns a null-terminated string in its character array argument. This means that when you use **gets( )**, you may type characters at the keyboard until you strike a carriage return. Striking a carriage return places a null terminator at the end of the string and **gets( )** returns. The carriage return itself is not contained in the string, and it is impossible to use **gets( )** to return a carriage return; **getchar( )** can do so, however. The **gets( )** allows you to correct mistakes by using the BACKSPACE key prior to pressing RETURN.

The **puts( )** function writes its string argument to the screen. A **puts( )** recognizes the same backslash codes as **printf( )**, such as \n for newline. A call to **puts( )** requires far less overhead than the same call to **printf( )** because **puts( )** only outputs a string of characters to the screen. It cannot output numbers or do format conversions. Therefore, **puts( )** takes up less space and runs faster than **printf( )** when displaying strings. Although a few compilers have neglected this function, **puts( )** is in most standard libraries. If you do not have a **puts( )** available, the simple one shown here will work. If you compare it to most **printf( )** functions, this **puts( )** is several times smaller:

```
puts(s)
char *s;
{
        register int t;

        for(t=0;s[t];++t) putchar(s[t]);
}
```

The **puts( )** function is important when code size is important. If a program does not require all of the functions of **printf( )**, it is to your advantage not to use a large function like **printf( )** when the simple **puts( )** function will do. For example, here is an improved version of the **getnum( )** function from the one shown in Chapter 3:

```
getnum() /* version 2 */
{
        char num[80],n;

        do {
                gets(num);
                if(!number(num)) {
                        puts("Must be number\n");
                        n=0;
                }
                else n=1;
        } while (!n);
        return(atoi(num));
}

number(s)
char *s;
{
        int t;

        for(t=0;s[t];++t) if(!isdigit(s[t])) return 0;
        return 1;
}
```

This version will force you to enter a number because the support function, **number( )**, verifies that all of the characters in the string **num** are digits. The use of **puts( )** instead of **printf( )** means that using **getnum( )** does not drag in the large function **printf( )**. Remember, if any function in your program requires **printf( )**, it will be loaded at link time, so it is important to use the smallest functions in standard functions.

Table 6-1. The Simplest Console I/O Functions

Function	Operation
getchar( )	Reads a character from the keyboard
putchar( )	Writes a character to the screen
gets( )	Reads a string from the keyboard
puts( )	Writes a string to the screen

The simplest functions that perform console I/O operations are summarized in Table 6-1.

Formatted Console I/O

In addition to the simple console I/O functions described in the previous section, the standard C library contains two functions that perform formatted output and input: **printf( )** and **scanf( )**. *Formatted I/O* refers to the fact that these functions may format the information under your direction. Remember, the simple routines described in the previous section will only input and display data in its raw form.

You are already somewhat familiar with **printf( )**. The complement of **printf( )**, **scanf( )**, allows the reading of various data types from the keyboard, including characters, strings, and numbers. Both **printf( )** and **scanf( )** allow the mixing of data formats and the use of, for example, field specifiers and decimal points.

The printf( ) Function

You can think of **printf( )** as a combination of BASIC's **PRINT** statement and its advanced **PRINT USING** statement. To summarize what you learned about **printf( )** in Chapter 2, the general form of **printf( )** is

printf("control string",argument list);

The control string consists of two types of items. The first type is made up of characters that will be printed on the screen. The second type contains format commands that define the way the subsequent arguments are displayed. There must be exactly the same number of format commands as there are arguments, and the format commands and the arguments are matched in order. For example, this **printf( )** call

```
printf("Hi %c %d %s",'c',10,"there!");
```

displays

```
Hi c 10 there!
```

Table 6-2. The Format Control Codes of **printf( )**

printf( ) code	Format
%c	A single character
%d	Decimal
%e	Scientific notation
%f	Decimal floating point
%g	Uses %e or %f, whichever is shorter
%o	Octal
%s	String of characters
%u	Unsigned decimal
%x	Hexadecimal

Table 6-2 relists the information given in Table 2-1 (in Chapter 2). The format control codes may have modifiers that specify the field width, the number of decimal places, and a left-justify flag. An integer placed between the % sign and the format command acts as a *minimum field-width specifier*. This pads the output with blanks or zeros to ensure that it is at least a certain minimum length. If the string or number is greater than that minimum, it will be printed in full even if it overruns the minimum. The default padding is done with spaces. If you wish to pad with zeros, you place a 0 before the field-width specifier. For example, **%05d** will pad a number of less than 5 digits with 0's.

To specify the number of decimal places printed for a floating point number, place a decimal point followed by the number of decimal points you wish to display after the field-width specifier. For example, **%10.4f** will display a number at least 10 characters wide with four decimal places. This method also works when you want to specify the maximum field length for strings and integer values. For example, **%5.7s** will display a string that will be at least five characters long and will not exceed seven. If the string is longer than the maximum field width, the characters will be truncated off the end.

By default, all output is *right-justified:* if the field width is larger than the data printed, the data will be placed on the right edge of the field. You can force the information to be displayed on the left by placing a minus sign directly after the %. For example, **%−10.2f** will left-justify a floating point number with two decimal places in a 10-character wide field.

The l modifier tells **printf( )** that a **long int** data type follows.

With **printf( )**, you can output virtually any format of data you desire, as

Table 6-3. Format Examples of **printf( )** Output

printf( ) statement	Output
("%−5.2f",123.234)	|123.23 |
("%5.2f",3.234)	| 3.23|
("%10s","hello")	| hello|
("%-10s","hello")	|hello |
("%5.7s","123456789")	| 1234567|

you can see in the examples in Table 6-3. By writing examples of your own and checking their results, you can see if you fully understand the process.

The scanf( ) Function

The function **scanf( )**, a general-purpose input routine, allows you to read formatted data and automatically convert numeric information into integers and **floats**, for example. It is much like the reverse of **printf( )**. The general form of **scanf( )** is

scanf(control string, argument list);

The control string is made up of input format codes, which are preceded by a % sign. These codes are listed in Table 6-4.

The format commands can use field-length modifiers that are integer numbers placed between the % and the format-command code. An * placed after the % will suppress the assignment and advance to the next input field.

Table 6-4. The **scanf( )** Format Codes

Code	Meaning
c	Read a single character
d	Read a decimal integer
e	Read a floating point number
f	Read a floating point number
h	Read a short integer
o	Read an octal number
s	Read a string
x	Read a hexadecimal number

Any other characters in the control string will be matched and discarded.

The input data items must be separated by spaces, tabs, or newlines. Punctuation marks like commas or semicolons do not count as separators. As in **printf( )**, the **scanf( )** format codes match the variables receiving the input in order.

All the variables used to receive values through **scanf( )** must be passed by their addresses. This means that all arguments, other than the control string, must be pointers to the variables that will receive input. Remember, this is C's way of creating a "call by reference." For example, if you wish to read an integer into the variable **count**, you would use this **scanf( )** call:

```
scanf("%d",&count);
```

Strings will be read into character arrays, and the array name, without any index, is the address of the first element of the array. Thus, to read a string into the character array **address**, you would use

```
scanf("%s",address);
```

In this case, **address** is already a pointer and need not be preceded by the **&** operator.

The *maximum field-length modifier* may be applied to the format codes. If you wish to read no more than 20 characters into **address**, you would write

```
scanf("%20s",address);
```

If the input stream were greater than 20 characters, a subsequent call to input would begin where this call left off. For example, if

```
1100 Parkway Ave, apt 2110 B
```

had been entered as the response to the earlier **scanf( )** call, only the first 20 characters, or up to the **p** in **apt**, would have been placed into **address** because of the maximum-size specifier. This means that the remaining 8 characters, **t 2110 B**, have not yet been used. If you make another **scanf( )** call, such as

```
scanf("%s",str);
```

then **t 2110 B** would be placed into **str**. However, many microcomputer operating systems would simply lose characters that were typed but not assigned to anything. Only if the system supports buffered I/O will those characters remain for processing.

Although spaces, tabs, and newlines are used as field separators, when a single character is being read, these are read like any other character. For example, with an input stream of **x y**,

```
scanf("%c%c%c",&a,&b,&c);
```

will return with the character **x** in **a**, a space in **b**, and the character **y** in **c**.

Be careful: if you have any other characters in the control string—including spaces, tabs, and newlines—those characters will be used to check against characters from the input stream. Any character that matches one of them will be discarded. For example, given the input stream **abcdtttttefg**,

```
scanf("%st%s",name1,name2);
```

will place the characters **abcd** into **name1** and the characters **efg** into **name2**. The t's are discarded because of the **t** in the control string. In another example,

```
scanf("%s ",name);
```

will *not* return until you type a character *after* you type a terminator: the space after %s has instructed **scanf( )** to read and discard spaces, tabs, and newline characters.

Unlike BASIC's **INPUT** statement, it is impossible to issue a prompt as part of the **scanf( )** call. The control string may not be used to output characters as it is in **printf( )**. Therefore, all prompts must be done explicitly prior to the **scanf( )** call.

The ability of **scanf( )** to process various types of data is frequently used in database programs. A short program that will keep a list of the last names and current balances of clients will be developed. This will help illustrate the use of formatted console I/O.

Using a top-down approach, you will first write the **main( )** function of the program. The program will arbitrarily be restricted to 50 clients. The last name of each client will be a maximum of 19 characters plus a null terminator, which is a 20-character total field length. There will be five procedures in the operation of the program. They are

• Enter a client

- Find and display a client

- Update a client

- Delete a client

- Exit the program.

A **switch( )** statement accesses these five procedures. Each entry in the **switch( )** calls the appropriate function to handle one of the options. Figure 6-2 shows how the **main( )** function looks in the client database program.

The first function that we will need is **init( )**, which initializes the database to all zeros:

```
init()
{
        register int t;
        for(t=0; t<1000;++t)
                name[t]='\0';
}
```

Filling the array **name** with nulls will simplify the functions that are used to manipulate this data. The reason **balance** is not initialized is that all references to the database are by the client's name, and the balance itself is also referenced by this name.

To enter data into the database, we will need the function **enter( )**:

```
enter()
{
        char s[20];
        int slot;

        for(slot=0;slot<50;slot++) {
                if(!name[slot*20]) break; /* found open one*/
        }
        if(slot==50) {
                printf("Client list full\n");
                return 0;
        }
        printf("Enter name and balance:\n");
        scanf("%19s%d",&name[slot*20],&balance[slot]);
}
```

The **enter( )** contains the first use of **scanf( )**. The **scanf( )** will read as many as 19 characters for the client's last name before reading the balance due.

```
char name[1000];   /* 50 client names, each 20 chars */
int balance[50];
main()  /* simple client database program */
{
        char ch;
        int client;
        init(); /* initialize the database to zero */
        do {    /*  main loop */
                printf("You may:\n");
                printf("\n\n    1. Enter a new client\n");
                printf("    2. Find a client\n");
                printf("    3. Update a client\n");
                printf("    4. Delete a client\n");
                printf("    5. Exit\n");
                do {
                        printf("Select one: ");
                        ch=getchar();
                } while(ch<'1' || ch >'5');
                printf("\n");
                switch(ch) {
                    case '1':
                        enter();
                        break;
                    case '2':
                        client=find();
                        if(client!=-1) display(client);
                        break;
                    case '3':
                        client=find();
                        if(client!=-1) update(client);
                        break;
                    case '4':
                        client=find();
                        if(client!=-1) delete(client);
                        break;
                    case '5':
                        break;
                }
        } while(ch!='5');
}
```

Figure 6-2. A client database program

Because **scanf( )** stops reading at a space, only the last name may be entered. You would need two variables in order to read the first and last names. For example, if the input from the keyboard for the first entry is

```
Johnston 123
```

name[0] would contain **Johnston' \0'** and **balance[0]** would be **123**.

After a name is entered, you can retrieve the current balance by searching on the client's last name. The first of two functions needed to do this is **find( )**, a general-purpose search function that returns the record number or **slot** of the data:

```
find()
{
        char s[20];
        int slot;
        printf("Enter client name:\n");
        scanf("%19s", s);
        for(slot=0;slot<50;slot++) {
                if(!strcmp(s,&name[slot*20])) break;
                        /* found it, so break loop */
        }
        if(slot==50) {
                printf("Client not in list.\n");
                return (-1);
        }
        return slot;
}
```

When the record number is known, the client name and balance can be displayed by using the second function, **display( )**:

```
display(slot)
int slot;
{
  printf("\n%s balance is %d\n",&name[slot*20],balance[slot]);
}
```

A client's information may be updated by calling **update( )** with the number of the record to be changed; **scanf( )** is used to enter the new information:

```
update(slot)
int slot;
{
        printf("Enter new name and balance:");
        scanf("%19s%d",&name[20*slot],&balance[slot]);
}
```

Notice that only a maximum of 19 characters will be read. This leaves room for the null terminator at the end.

We can easily delete a client from the database by using **delete( )**, which places a null in the first character position of the **slot**:

```
delete(slot)
int slot;
{
        printf("slot deleted\n");
        name[20*slot]='\0';
        balance[slot]=0;
}
```

If you enter and compile these functions, you can have fun playing with this program and adding functions here or there to do something new.

Reading and Writing Files

Very few useful programs exist that do not read and write data files. In the client database from the previous section, all data is lost when the program is terminated. This is a serious limitation of its usefulness. In this section, you will learn how to read and write a disk file.

There are basically two distinct ways to read and write disk files in C. The first way is high-level I/O: all reads and writes are done a character at a time. This is sometimes called *buffered I/O* because you do not have to worry about sector sizes, buffer lengths, and other operating system-dependent considerations. In other words, these functions provide their own buffering. The second way is low-level I/O, which is sometimes called *UNIX-like*. In this method, you must perform each read and write manually, providing your own buffers, counters, and pointers.

Header Files

Before you can learn about disk I/O, a short digression will have to be made. C supports two statements that greatly simplify certain aspects of programming. The first is **#define**, which is used to define a string of characters as a constant. For example, this statement makes the string **MAX—NUM** stand for 100:

```
#define MAX_NUM 100
```

Notice that no equal sign is used and that the statement *does not* end in a semicolon.

The **#define** statement forces the compiler to make a macro substitution — in this case the number 100 — each time the string **MAX—NUM** is encountered. A *macro substitution* is simply the replacement of one piece of text for another as your program is being compiled. In the case of strings, the macro is often shorter and easier to work with in your program. In the case of numbers, using the macro allows you to easily change a constant used throughout your program by changing it in its **#define** statement. Using names instead of numbers adds meaning to those constants and helps the reader of the program better understand what is happening. You could then legally write

$$for(t=0;t<MAX—NUM;++t) \ldots$$

You may also use **#define** to perform macro substitutions on strings, such as

```
#define err1    "Syntax error"
```

You could then legally write the statement

```
printf(err1);
```

The second statement you need to know is **#include**. This is used at compile time to read another source file, usually header information, into your program. For example, if you have several files for a program called **spreadsheet**, you might want to create a standard header file containing all of the global variables needed by the separate files. If you called this file **spreadsheet.h**, the following statement would be the first line in your program:

```
#include "spreadsheet.h"
```

The reason that **#include** and **#define** have been discussed here is that you will need them to use the disk file functions supplied with your compiler. Each file that will use disk I/O will require that you read in a header file called **stdio.h**, which is provided by your C compiler's developers. It must be on the same disk that your program files are on. You should place the line

```
#include "stdio.h"
```

near the first line of each program file. This file will not only define certain system-dependent data structures, but will also define certain macros, such as **EOF** for end-of-file marker. Your C compiler manual should tell you exactly what macros are defined and available for your use.

High-Level File I/O

In the C high-level I/O system, there are five essential functions. They are

- **fopen( )**, which opens a file for use

- **putc( )**, which writes a character to a file

- **getc( )**, which reads a character from a file

- **fclose( )**, which closes a file

- **fseek( )**, which is used to perform random disk operations.

The *fopen( )* Function

The function **fopen( )** serves two functions: first, it opens a disk file for use and, second, it returns a file pointer. The general form of **fopen( )** is

> FILE *fp;
>
> fp = fopen(filename,mode);

where mode is a string containing either **r** for read, **w** for write, or **a** for append. Usually the read/write mode is specified with the string **rw**. (Your compiler may have additional modes, so check your user manual.) The filename must be a string of characters that make up a valid filename for the operating system.

The variable **fp** is of type **FILE** and is the file pointer. **FILE** is a specific data type defined in **stdio.h** for you by your compiler's implementor. All file pointers must be declared to be of type **FILE**. (A few compilers may call this data type by a different name, so check your documentation.)

If you wished to open a file for writing with the name **test**, you would write

```
fp = fopen("test","w");
```

However, you will usually see it written like this:

```
If ((fp = fopen("test","w"))==NULL) {
    puts("cannot open file\n");
    exit();
}
```

This method detects any error in opening a file, such as a write-protected or a full disk, before attempting to write to it. A null, which is usually 0, is used because no file pointer will ever have the value 0.

If you use **fopen( )** to open a file for write, any pre-existing file by that name will be erased and a new file started. If you want to add to the end of the file, you must use mode **a**.

The putc( ) Function

The **putc( )** function is used to write characters to a disk file that was opened using the **fopen( )** function with mode **w**. The general form of the function is

putc(c,fp);

where **fp** is the file pointer returned by **fopen( )** and **c** is the character to be output. The file pointer tells **putc( )** which disk file to write to.

The *getc( ) Function*

The function **getc( )** is used to read characters from a file opened in read mode by **fopen( )**. The general form of the function is

```
char ch;
ch = getc(fp);
```

where **fp** is a file pointer of type **FILE** returned by **fopen( )**. The file pointer tells **getc( )** which file to read from.

   The **getc( )** will return an end-of-file marker when the end of the file has been reached. The header file **stdio.h** will use #**define** to create the macro **EOF** that will be the end-of-file marker. Therefore, to read until the end-of-file marker, you could use the following code:

```
ch = getc(fp);
while(ch!=EOF) {
    .
    .
    .
    ch=getc(fp);
}
```

Since the EOF marker may not be a printing character, do not try to print it on your screen.

The *fclose( ) Function*

The function **fclose( )** is used to close a file that was opened by a call to **fopen( )**. *You must close all files before your program terminates.* The **fclose( )** does more than just free the file pointer; it writes any data not yet written to the disk and does a formal operating system-level close on the file. Failure to close a file invites all kinds of trouble, including lost data, destroyed files, and possible intermittent errors in your program.

   The general form of the **fclose( )** function call is

```
fclose(fp);
```

where **fp** is the file pointer returned by the call to **fopen( )**.

Using *fopen( )*, *getc( )*, *putc( )*, and *fclose( )*

Before learning about **fseek( )**, you will see how the individual functions that make up high-level I/O work together.

A simple example of using **fopen( )**, **putc( )**, and **fclose( )** is the program **ktod** given in Figure 6-3. (The next program will include **getc( )**.) It simply reads characters from the keyboard and writes them to a disk file until a > is typed. The filename is specified from the command line.

In **ktod**, the macros **CR** and **LF** were defined (using **#define**) as being their decimal values, so that when a return was typed at the keyboard, the proper carriage return/line feed sequence could be put in the disk file. Without this step, only the line feed (or carriage return on some systems) would have been written to the disk file.

```
#include "stdio.h"
#define CR      13
#define LF      10
main(argc,argv)  /* ktod - key to disk */
int argc;
char *argv[];
{
        FILE *fp;
        char ch;
        if(argc!=2) {
                printf("You forgot to enter the filename\n");
                exit(0);
        }
        if((fp=fopen(argv[1],"w"))  == NULL) {
                printf("cannot open file\n");
                exit(0);
        }
        do {
                ch=getchar();
                if(ch=='\n') {
                        putc(CR,fp);   /* put out cr/lf combo */
                        putc(LF,fp);
                }
                else  putc(ch,fp);
        } while (ch!='>');
        fclose(fp);
}
```

Figure 6-3. The program **ktod**, which uses **fopen( )**, **putc( )**, and **fclose( )**

```
#include "stdio.h"
main(argc,argv)      /* dtos - disk to screen */
int argc;
char *argv[];
{
        FILE *fp;
        char ch;
        if(argc!=2) {
                printf("You forgot to enter the filename\n");
                exit(0);
        }
        if((fp=fopen(argv[1],"r")) == NULL) {
                printf("cannot open file\n");
                exit(0);
        }
        ch=getc(fp);     /* read one character */
        while (ch!=EOF) {
                putchar(ch);      /* print on screen */
                ch=getc(fp);
        }
        fclose(fp);
}
```

Figure 6-4. The program **dtos**, which makes use of **getc( )**

Using **getc( )**, the complementary program **dtos**, listed in Figure 6-4, will read any ASCII file and display the contents on the screen.

The C high-level I/O functions and their operations hardly resemble BASIC disk operations. However, if you know BASIC, the BASIC version of **ktod** and **dtos** are shown in Figure 6-5 and Figure 6-6. There will be slight

```
10 INPUT F$ : REM KTOD - KEY TO DISK
20 OPEN F$ FOR OUTPUT AS #1
30 INPUT A$
60 PRINT #1,A$
80 IF A$=">" THEN 90 ELSE GOTO 30
90 CLOSE #1
100 END
```

Figure 6-5. The BASIC version of **ktod**

```
10 INPUT F$ : REM DTOS - DISK TO SCREEN
20 OPEN F$ FOR INPUT AS #1
30 IF EOF(1) THEN CLOSE:END
40 INPUT #1, A$
50 PRINT A$
60 GOTO 30
```

Figure 6-6.   The BASIC version of **dtos**

differences in the way they operate because BASIC does not easily emulate C's character-oriented I/O system. The names of the files are entered at run-time, instead of on the command line, because most BASICs do not allow command-line arguments. Instead of being able to type a > at any time as in the C version, the > must be the only character on a line in the BASIC version.

The *fseek( )* Function

You can perform random read and write operations using the high-level I/O system with the help of **fseek( )**. The **fseek( )** is used to set the current (specified byte) position in a file. The general form of the function is

fseek(fp, offset, origin);

where **fp** is a file pointer returned by a call to **fopen( )**, the **offset** is the number of bytes from the **origin** to make the current position, and the **origin** is either a 0 for the start of the file, a 1 for the current position, or a 2 for the end-of-file.

For example, if you wanted to read the 234th byte in a file called **test**, you could use this:

```
func1()
{
    FILE *fp;
    if((fp=fopen("test","r")) == NULL) {
        printf("cannot open file\n");
        exit(1);
    }
    fseek(fp,234,0);
    return getc(fp);              /* read one character */
                                  /* at 234th position */
}
```

The getw( ) and putw( ) Functions

In addition to **getc( )** and **putc( )**, most C compilers support two additional high-level I/O functions: **getw( )** and **putw( )**. They are used to read and write two-byte integers to and from a disk file.

The functions **getc( )** and **putc( )** can only operate on characters. How, then, can a two-byte integer be read or written from a disk file? The answer is to read/write both bytes that form the integer. The easiest way is to use the functions **getw( )** and **putw( )**. These functions work exactly the same as **getc( )** and **putc( )** except that instead of writing a single character, they write a two-byte integer. For example, you could modify the **ktod** program to place a character count at the end of the file. This program, listed in Figure 6-7, will be called **ktodc**.

In order to read files written by **ktodc**, you will need to modify **dtos** so that it will read the count at the end of the file and look for the file terminator $>$ as a signal to read the count. The new program **dtosc** is shown in Figure 6-8.

The program **dtosc** will work with most files as long as there is either a $>$ and a count at the end or if the $>$ is not in the file. You could alter the exact character used to signal the end of text, but what is important here is the concept. Do not confuse the $>$ used to signal the end of text with the **EOF** marker. The **EOF** is a standard marker defined by your C compiler. We have used the $>$ as an arbitrary method of telling **dtosc** that the text has ended and that the count is the next thing in the file.

If your C compiler's library does not have a **putw( )** or a **getw( )** function, you can use the simple version shown here:

```
putw(i,fp)
int i;
FILE *fp;
{
        char *t;

        t=&i;   /* assign the address of i to char *t */
        putc(t[0],fp);
        putc(t[1],fp);
}

getw(fp)
char *fp;
{
        char *t;
        int i;
```

```
        t=&i;   /* let char *t have address of int i */
        t[0]=getc(fp);
        t[1]=getc(fp);
        return(i);  /* note, return i not t !!!! */
}
```

Neither of these functions as shown provides any error checking. However, you can add this capability if you want.

The general idea behind **getw( )** and **putw( )** is that integers are really two bytes wide. Therefore, the integer can be broken into two bytes, as in

```
#include "stdio.h"
#define CR      13
#define LF      10
main(argc,argv)  /* ktodc - key to disk with count*/
int argc;
char *argv[];
{
    FILE *fp;
    char ch;
    int count;
    count = 0;
    if(argc!=2) {
            printf("You forgot to enter the filename\n");
            exit(0);
    }
    if((fp=fopen(argv[1],"w")) == NULL) {
            printf("cannot open file\n");
            exit(0);
    }
    do {
            ch=getchar();
            if(ch=='\n') {
                    putc(CR,fp);   /* put out cr/lf combo */
                    putc(LF,fp);
                    count++;
            }
            else  putc(ch,fp);
            count++;
    } while (ch!='>');
    putw(count,fp); /* write character count to disk */
    fclose(fp);
}
```

Figure 6-7.   The program **ktodc**, which uses **getw( )** and **putw( )**

```
#include "stdio.h"
main(argc,argv)      /* dtosc - disk to screen with count */
int argc;
char *argv[];
{
    FILE *fp;
    char ch;
    int count;
    if(argc!=2) {
            printf("You forgot to enter the filename\n");
            exit(0);
    }
    if((fp=fopen(argv[1],"r")) == NULL) {
            printf("cannot open file\n");
            exit(0);
    }
    ch=getc(fp);     /* read one character */
    while (ch!=EOF && ch!='>') {  /* look for '>' signal */
            putchar(ch);     /* print on screen */
            ch=getc(fp);
    }
    if(ch=='>') {
            count=getw(fp);
            printf("character count is: %d",count);
    }
    fclose(fp);
}
```

Figure 6-8. The program **dtosc**, an adaptation of the program dtos

putw( ), by assigning its address to a character pointer and writing each byte at a time using **putc( )**. The reverse is also true: an integer can be reconstructed a byte at a time by assigning its address to a character pointer and performing two successive **getc( )** calls.

Reading and Writing Other Data Types

Most C libraries will not have built-in functions to read and write any data types other than character and integer. However, you may write these other data types by constructing functions that operate in ways similar to **getw( )** and **putw( )**.

For example, if data of type **float** were eight bytes in length, this function, **putfloat( )**, could be used to write a floating point number to a disk file:

```
putfloat(num,fp)
float num;
FILE *fp;
{
        char *t;
        int count;

        t = &num;
        for(count=0; count<8; +=count)
                putc(t[count],fp);
}
```

In fact, you could construct specific **put_x( )** and **get_x( )** functions where **x** is any arbitrary data structure or unit. It need not be limited to predefined data types only.

The *stdin, stdout,* and *stderr* Files

When every C program starts execution, three files are opened automatically: *standard input,* or **stdin**; *standard output,* or **stdout**; and *standard error,* or **stderr**. Normally, these refer to the console. They are, however, file pointers and may be used by the high-level I/O system to perform I/O operations on the console. In essence, they allow the console to be treated as if it were a file. For example, **putchar( )** could be defined as

```
putchar(c)
char c;
{
        putc(c,stdout);
}
```

In general, **stdin** is used to read from the console, and **stdout** and **stderr** are used to write to the console. In operating systems that support redirection of I/O, only **stdin** and **stdout** will be redirected, with **stderr** still writing to the console. (This will vary with each operating system and C implementation, so check your user's manual.)

You may use **stdin, stdout,** and **stderr** as file pointers in any function that used a variable of type ***FILE.**

Remember that **stdin**, **stdout**, and **stderr** are not variables but constants, and as such may not be assigned to or altered. Just as these file pointers are created automatically at the start of your program, they are closed automatically at the end; you should not try to use **fclose( )** to close them.

The *fprintf( )* and *fscanf( )* Functions

In addition to the basic I/O functions of **getc( )** and **putc( )**, the libraries of most C implementations have **fprintf( )** and **fscanf( )**, which can be used to write various data formats to a file opened by **fopen( )**. The general form of **fprintf( )** is

> fprintf(fp, control string, argument list);

and the general form of **fscanf( )** is

> fscanf(fp, control string, argument list);

where **fp** is a file pointer returned by a call to **fopen( )**. Except for directing their output to the file defined by **fp**, **fprintf( )** and **fscanf( )** operate exactly like **printf( )** and **scanf( )**, respectively.

To illustrate how useful these functions can be, the program in Figure 6-9 will read information from the keyboard, write it to a disk file, and then read and display the information back on the screen.

A word of warning: although **fprintf( )** and **fscanf( )** often are the easiest way to write and read disk files, they are not the most efficient, because ASCII data is being written just as it appears on your screen instead of in binary. If you are concerned with speed or file size, you should probably write custom file routines similar to **putw( )** and **getw( )**.

Low-Level I/O:
The Unix-like File Routines

Because C was originally developed under the UNIX operating system and because certain applications require the ability to command the disk operations at the operating-system level, a second disk file I/O subsystem was

```
main()   /* fscanf - fprintf example */
{
        FILE *fp;
        char s[80];
        int t;
        if((fp=fopen("test","w")) == NULL) {
                printf("cannot open file\n");
                exit(0);
        }
        fscanf(stdin,"%s%d",s,&t);   /* read from keyboard */

        fprintf(fp,"%s %d",s,t);    /* write to file */

        fclose(fp);

        if((fp=fopen("test","r")) == NULL) {

                printf("cannot open file\n");

                exit(0);

        }

        fscanf(fp,"%s%d",s,&t);   /* read from file */

        fprintf(stdout,"%s %d",s,t); /* printf on

                                        screen */

}
```

Figure 6-9. A program that uses **fprintf( )** and **fscanf( )**

created. It uses functions that are separate from those you learned about in the previous sections. These are the low-level, UNIX-like disk I/O functions:

**read( )   write( )   open( )
close( )   creat( )   unlink( )
lseek( )**

The reason that the disk I/O subsystem made up of these functions is called "low-level" is that, as the programmer, you must provide and maintain *all* disk buffers. Unlike the functions **getc( )** and **putc( )**, which wrote and read characters from or to a stream of data that was automatically written to or read from a disk file, the functions **read( )** and **write( )** will read or write one complete buffer of information with each call. You must place the information to be used into this buffer, and you must know when the buffer is full. You define the buffer and record lengths for your file.

Beginners in C will usually find the high-level I/O system easier to work with and less prone to error. However, as you advance, the low-level I/O system can offer more flexibility and speed for certain applications.

The *open( )*, *close( )*, And *creat( )* Functions

Unlike the high-level I/O system, the low-level system does not use file pointers of type **FILE**, but rather file descriptors of type **int**. The general form of a call to **open( )** is

```
int fd;
fd = open(filename, mode);
```

where filename is any valid filename and mode is one of the following integers:

Mode	Effect
0	read
1	write
2	read/write

The **open( )** function returns a −1 if the file cannot be opened. You will, however, usually see the call to **open( )** like this:

```
int fd;
if((fd=open(filename, mode)) == -1)  {
        printf("cannot open file\n");
        exit(0);
}
```

Depending upon the exact implementation of your C compiler, you may be able to use **open( )** to create a file that is currently nonexistent. You should check your user manual.

The general form for **close( )** is

```
int fd;
close(fd);
```

The **close( )** function returns a −1 if it is unable to close the file. This could occur if the diskette was removed from the drive, for example.

The **close( )** function releases the file descriptor, so that it can be reused for another file. There is always some limit to the number of open files that may exist simultaneously, so you should use **close( )** on a file when it is no longer needed. Although normal program termination also closes all files automatically, this is not considered good programming practice.

If your compiler does not allow you to create a new file using **open( )**, or if you want to ensure portability, you will have to use **creat( )**. The **creat( )** function essentially opens a new file for write operations. The general form of **creat( )** is

```
int fd;
fd = creat(filename, pmode);
```

where filename is any valid filename. The pmode is not used with most microcomputer-based C compilers, although it will still be part of the **creat( )** call. (Consult your C user manual for specific details.) Essentially, pmode has to do with protection modes under UNIX. A **creat( )** returns a −1 on failure.

The *write( )* and *read( )* Functions

Once a file has been opened for writing and you have declared a character array to act as a buffer, your file may be accessed by **write( )**. With each write operation, the buffer will be written to disk. You will also need to specify the buffer size: this is the number of bytes actually written to the disk file. Generally, this should be the same as the size of your buffer. In some systems, this must be an even multiple of 128. In others, it may be any number. Be certain to check your C user manual.

The general form of the **write( )** function is

```
#define BUF_SIZE      128
int fd;
char buf[BUF_SIZE];
write(fd,buf,BUF_SIZE);
```

Each time that a call to **write( )** is executed, the characters designated by **BUF—SIZE** are written to the disk file specified by **fd** from the character array **buf**. The character array **buf** does not need to be null-terminated because it is not a string.

You might be wondering why the entire contents of the buffer aren't automatically written to disk. The answer is that the buffer may not be null-terminated. There is no way for the **write( )** function to know how long the buffer is without being told explicitly. You may also wish to write less than a full buffer.

The **write( )** function will return the buffer size after a successful write operation. Upon failure, most implementations will return a −1, but check your user manual.

The **read( )** function is the complement of **write( )**. The general form of **read( )** is

$$\text{read(fd, buf, BUF\_SIZE);}$$

where **fd**, **buf**, and **BUF—SIZE** are the same as for **write( )**. If **read( )** is successful, it returns the number of characters actually read. It will return 0 upon the physical end-of-file, and −1 if errors occur.

The program shown in Figure 6-10 illustrates some aspects of low-level I/O. It will read lines of text from the keyboard and write them to a disk file. After they are written, the program will read them back.

The *unlink( )* Function

If you wish to remove a file from the directory, you would use **unlink( )**. Although **unlink( )** is considered part of the low-level I/O system, it will remove any file from the directory. The general form of **unlink( )** is

$$\text{unlink(filename);}$$

where filename is a character pointer to any valid filename. The **unlink( )** function will return an error (usually −1) if it was unable to erase the file. This could happen if the file was not present on the diskette to begin with or if the diskette was write-protected.

```
#include "stdio.h"
#define BUF_SIZE        128
main()  /* read and write using low-level I/O */
{
        char buf[BUF_SIZE];
        int fd1, fd2, t;
        if((fd1=open("test",1))==-1) { /* open for write */
                printf("cannot open file \n");
                exit(0);
        }
        input(buf,fd1);
        /* now close file and read back */
        close(fd1);
        if((fd2=open("test",0))==-1) { /* open for write */
                printf("cannot open file \n");
                exit(0);
        }
        display(buf,fd2);
        close(fd2);
}
input(buf,fd1)
char *buf;
int fd1;
{
        do {
                gets(buf); /* input chars from keyboard
                if(write(fd1,buf,BUF_SIZE)!=BUF_SIZE) {
                        printf("error on write \n");
                        exit(0);
                }
        } while (!strcmp(buf,"quit"));
}
display(buf,fd2)
char *buf;
int fd2;
{
        do {
                gets(buf); /* input chars from keyboard */
                if(read(fd2,buf,BUF_SIZE) < 0) {
                        printf("error on write \n");
                        exit(0);
                }
                printf(buf);
        } while (!strcmp(buf,"quit"));
}
```

Figure 6-10. A program that reads lines of text from the keyboard and
writes them to a disk file

Table 6-5.   The Effect of the Origin on **lseek**

Origin	Effect of call to lseek( )
0	Count the offset from the start of the file
1	Count the offset from the current position
2	Count the offset from the end of the file

Random-Access Files and *lseek( )*

C supports random-access file I/O under the low-level I/O system by using calls to **lseek( )**. The general form of **lseek( )** is

```
int fd, origin;
long offset;
lseek(fd, offset, origin);
```

where **fd** is a file descriptor returned by a **creat( )** or **open( )** call.

The way that **lseek( )** works depends on the values of the origin and the offset. The origin may be either a 0, 1, or 2. Table 6-5 explains how the offset is interpreted for each origin value.

A simple example using **lseek( )** is the program **read_file** shown in Figure 6-11. To run it, you must specify a file from the command line. You may then specify the specific buffer you wish to read. Entering a negative number will allow you to exit. You may want to change the buffer size to match the sector size of your system, although it is not necessary.

Using Disk Files

In this section, disk file read and write routines will be added to the client database program in Figure 6-2. This will enable you to save the database in a disk file and read it back at a later time.

The first routine that needs to be written is called **wr_data( )**, which

```
#include "stdio.h"
#define BUF_SIZE         128
main(argc,argv) /* read and write using low-level I/O */
int argc;
char *argv[];
{
        char buf[BUF_SIZE+1],s[10];
        int fd, sector;
        buf[BUF_SIZE+1]='\0'; /* null terminate buffer for printf  */
        if((fd=open(argv[1],0))==-1) { /* open for write */
                printf("cannot open file \n");
                exit(0);
        }
        do {
                gets(s);
                sector=atoi(s); /* get the sector to read */
                if(lseek(fd,sector*BUF_SIZE,0)==-1)
                        printf("seek error \n");
                if(read(fd,buf,BUF_SIZE)==0) {
                        printf("sector out of range\n");
                }
                else
                        printf(buf);
        } while(sector>0);
        close(fd);
}
```

Figure 6-11.   The program **read—file**, which uses **lseek( )**

writes the entire database to a file called **client** and uses the high-level I/O
system:

```
wr_data()
{
    register int t;
    FILE *fp;

    if((fp=fopen("client","w"))==0) {
            printf("cannot open client file\n");
            exit(0);
    }
    for(t=0;t<1000;t++) {
            putc(name[t],fp);  /* save the clients names */
    }
    for(t=0;t<50;++t) {
            putw(balance[t],fp);  /* save the balances */
    }
    fclose(fp);
}
```

The second routine that you need is **rd—data( )**, which will read the entire database from the **client** file and which also uses the high-level I/O system:

```
rd_data()
{
    register int t;
    FILE *fp;

    if((fp=fopen("client","r"))==0) {
            printf("cannot open client file\n");
            exit(0);
    }
    for(t=0;t<1000;t++) {
            name[t]=getc(fp);   /* save the clients names */
    }
    for(t=0;t<50;++t) {
            balance[t]=getw(fp);   /* save the balances */
    }
    fclose(fp);
}
```

```
#include "stdio.h"
char name[1000];   /* 50 client names, each 20 chars */
int balance[50];
main()  /* simple client database program */
{
        char ch;
        int client;
        init(); /* initialize the database to zero */
        do {    /* main loop */
                printf("You may: \n");
                printf("\n\n    1. Enter a new client\n");
                printf("    2. Find a client\n");
                printf("    3. Update a client\n");
                printf("    4. Delete a client\n");
                printf("    5. Save the database \n");
                printf("    6. Load the database \n");
                printf("    7. Exit\n");
                do {
                        printf("Select one: ");
                        ch=getchar();
                } while(ch<'1' || ch >'7');
                printf("\n");
                switch(ch) {
```

Figure 6-12. The new version of the client database program given in Figure 6-2

```
                        case '1':
                            enter();
                            break;
                        case '2':
                            client=find();
                            if(client!=-1) display(client);
                            break;
                        case '3':
                            client=find();
                            if(client!=-1) update(client);
                            break;
                        case '4':
                            client=find();
                            if(client!=-1) delete(client);
                            break;
                        case '5':
                            wr_data();
                            break;
                        case '6':
                            rd_data();
                            break;
                        case 7:
                            break;
                    }
            } while(ch!='7');
}
```

Figure 6-12. The new version of the client database program given in
Figure 6-2 (*continued*)

Finally, Figure 6-12 shows the modified **main( )** function to include the
two new options.

In summary, the C standard library actually contains two separate file
I/O systems: the high-level and the low-level. Although either system can be
used for any task, each has its own relative merits. The good C programmer
will choose the right system for the job. In general, the low-level routines are
faster but may require more work on your part. You should first consult your
C user manual for details before using any of the disk file functions.

E X E R C I S E S

1. Write a short program that will emulate a four-function calculator. For each calculation, input two numbers and an operator. Using a **switch** statement based on the operator, print the outcome of the operation. For example, if you input 100 100 +, you would print 200 on the screen.

2. Write a **printf( )** call that will display at least 5 characters, but not more than 10 characters, for each of these types of data: string, integer, and float.

3. Write a **scanf( )** call that will input a string and two integer numbers.

4. Write a program using high-level I/O that will copy one disk file to another. Use command-line arguments to specify the files.

5. Modify the client database example so that it stores both first and last names.

6. Modify the client database file routines to store and retrieve both the first and last names that you added in the previous exercise.

A N S W E R S

1.
```
#include "stdio.h"

main()   /* calc program */
{
        float num1, num2;
        char op;

        do {
                printf("enter two numbers and operator: ");
                scanf("%f%f %c",&num1,&num2,&op);
                switch(op) {
                    case '+':
                        printf("%f\n",num1+num2);
                        break;
                    case '-':
                        printf("%f\n",num1-num2);
                        break;
                    case '/':
                        printf("%f\n",num1/num2);
                        break;
                    case '*':
                        printf("%f\n",num1*num2);
                        break;
                    default:
                        printf("Unknown operator\n");
                }
        } while(op!='q');
}
```

2.
```
printf("%5.10d %5.10s %5.10f",dec,string,flt);
```

3.
```
scanf("%s%d%d",s,d1,d2);
```

4.
```
#include "stdio.h"

main(argc,argv) /* copy program */
int argc;
char *argv[];
{
        char ch;
        FILE *fp1,*fp2;

        if((fp1=fopen(argv[1],"r"))==0) {
                printf("cannot open file %s\n",argv[1]);
                exit(0);
        }
        if((fp2=fopen(argv[2],"w"))==0) {
                printf("cannot open file %s\n",argv[2]);
                exit(0);
```

```
        }
        while((ch=getc(fp1))!=EOF) putc(ch,fp2);
        fclose(fp1); fclose(fp2);
}
```

5.
```
#include "stdio.h"
char name[1000];  /* 50 client names, each 20 chars */
char fname[1000]; /* hold the first names */
int balance[50];

main()  /* simple client database program */
{
        char ch;
        int client;

        init(); /* initialize the database to zero */

        do {    /*  main loop */
                printf("You may:\n");
                printf("\n\n    1. Enter a new client\n");
                printf("    2. Find a client\n");
                printf("    3. Update a client\n");
                printf("    4. Delete a client\n");
                printf("    5. Save the database\n");
                printf("    6. Load the database\n");
                printf("    7. Exit\n");
                do {
                        printf("Select one: ");
                        ch=getchar();
                } while(ch<'1' || ch >'7');
                printf("\n");

                switch(ch) {
                    case '1':
                        enter();
                        break;
                    case '2':
                        client=find();
                        if(client!=-1) display(client);
                        break;
                    case '3':
                        client=find();
                        if(client!=-1) update(client);
                        break;
                    case '4':
                        client=find();
                        if(client!=-1) delete(client);
                        break;
                    case '5':
                        wr_data();
                        break;
                    case '6':
                        rd_data();
                        break;
                    case '7':
                        break;
                }
        } while(ch!='7');
}
```

```
init()
{
        register int t;

        for(t=0; t<1000;++t)
                name[t]='\0';
}

enter()
{
        char s[20];
        int slot;

        for(slot=0;slot<50;slot++) {
                if(!name[slot*20]) break; /* found open one*/
        }
        if(slot==50) {
                printf("Client list full\n");
                return 0;
        }
        printf("Enter first and last name and balance:\n");
        scanf("%19s%19s%d",&fname[slot*20],&name[slot*20],&balance[slot]);
}

find()
{
        char s[20];
        int slot;

        printf("Enter client name:\n");
        scanf("%19s", s);
        for(slot=0;slot<50;slot++) {
                if(!strcmp(s,&name[slot*20])) break;
                        /* found it, so break loop */
        }
        if(slot==50) {
                printf("Client not in list.\n");
                return (-1);
        }
        return slot;
}

display(slot)
int slot;
{
        printf("\n%s %s  balance is %d\n",&fname[slot*20],&name[slot*20],ba
}

update(slot)
int slot;

{
        printf("Enter new name and balance:");
        scanf("%19s%19s%d",&fname[slot*20],&name[20*slot],&balance[slot]);
}

delete(slot)
int.slot;
{
        printf("slot deleted\n");
        name[20*slot]='\0';
        balance[slot]=0;
}
```

```
wr_data()
{
        register int t;
        FILE *fp;

        if((fp=fopen("client","w"))==0) {
                printf("cannot open client file\n");
                exit(0);
        }
        for(t=0;t<1000;t++) {
                putc(name[t],fp);  /* save the clients names */
        }
        for(t=0;t<1000;t++) {
                putc(fname[t],fp);  /* save the first names */
        }
        for(t=0;t<50;++t) {
                putw(balance[t],fp);  /* save the balances */
        }
        fclose(fp);
}

rd_data()
{
        register int t;
        FILE *fp;

        if((fp=fopen("client","r"))==0) {
                printf("cannot open client file\n");
                exit(0);
        }
        for(t=0;t<1000;t++) {
                name[t]=getc(fp);  /* save the clients names */
        }
        for(t=0;t<1000;t++) {
                fname[t]=getc(fp);  /* save the clients names */
        }
        for(t=0;t<50;++t) {
                balance[t]=getw(fp);  /* save the balances */
        }
        fclose(fp);
}
```

Pointers

C H A P T E R 7

You have already been introduced to pointers in previous chapters. In this chapter you will learn how to use pointers in greater detail and some tricks that will enable your programs to run faster. Pointer usage is very important to successful C programming, so read this chapter carefully.

C pointers do not parallel any structure in BASIC. It is possible to simulate them by using calls to **PEEK** and **POKE**, but seeing examples of these would probably not help you understand pointers. Therefore, no comparisons to BASIC will be made in this chapter.

Pointers as Addresses

A *pointer* is a variable that contains an address. Remember, this address is a location of another variable in memory. The value of a pointer "points" to a variable, which may be accessed indirectly with the special pointer operators

* and &. The * operator accesses the contents of a variable whose address is the value of a pointer. The * can be remembered as "at address." The & operator returns the address of a variable and can be remembered as "the address of."

For example, if **xyz** and **k** are integer variables and **h** is an integer pointer, then

```
h = &xyz;
k = *h;
```

assigns the value of **xyz** to **k**.

Pointers must be declared. To declare a pointer to an integer **x**, you would use

```
int *x;
```

For a **float** pointer **x**, you would use

```
float *x;
```

You must make sure that your pointer variables always point to the correct type of data. When you declare a pointer to be of type **int**, the compiler then assumes that any address that the pointer will hold will point to an integer variable. Because C allows you to assign any address to a pointer variable, the following code fragment will compile without errors but not produce the desired result:

```
float x,y;
int     *p;

p = &x;
y = *p;
```

This code *will not* assign the value of **x** to **y**. Because **p** is declared to be an integer pointer, only two bytes of information will be transferred to **y**, not the eight bytes that normally make up a floating point number.

As you saw in Chapter 6, this ability to assign any address to a pointer of any type is an advantage when reading and writing files. When you do this, you must be sure that you really know what you are doing. If your program gives you unexpected results, you should check your pointer assignments.

Pointer Assignments

As with any variable, a pointer may be used in the right side of assignment statements to assign its value to another pointer or to a nonpointer, as shown here:

```
int x;
unsigned y;
int *p1,p2;

p1 = &x;
p2 = p1;          /* give the address to x to p2 */
y = p2;
printf(" %u",y); /* print the decimal value of the
                    address of x - - not x's value!*/
```

You could have printed the decimal value of **p2** directly by using **p2** in the **printf( )** call. This code fragment is not meant to imply that unsigned integers are pointers or may be used to hold pointer values in general. Instead, it shows that a pointer value is simply a value like any other and may be assigned to any other variable type depending on conversion rules. Integers and pointers of any type are not interchangeable.

Pointer Expressions

Pointers may be used in most valid C expressions. Certain rules apply, and you may have to use additional parentheses to get the outcome that you want.

Pointer Arithmetic

There are only two arithmetic operators that may be used on pointers, + and −. To understand what occurs in pointer arithmetic, let **p1** be a pointer to an integer with a current value of 2000. After the expression

```
p1++;
```

The contents of **p1** will be 2002, not 2001. Each time **p1** is incremented, it will point to the *next integer*, which on most computers is two bytes wide. The same holds true of decrements. For example,

```
p1--;
```

will cause **p1** to have the value 1998, assuming that it previously was 2000.

Remember that each time a pointer is incremented, it will point to the memory location of the next element of its type. Each time it is decremented, it will point to the location of the previous element of its type.

For pointers to characters this will often appear as "normal" arithmetic. However, all other pointers will increase or decrease by the length of the data type that they point to. For integers, that length is usually two bytes; for **floats**, it will usually be eight. Although actual memory addresses were used in the explanation of how the various types of pointers differ, keep in mind that you will not need to know the actual values of pointers because they are not necessary in order to use them.

You are not limited to incrementing and decrementing pointers, however. You also may add integers to or subtract integers from pointers. The expression

```
p1 = p1 + 9;
```

will make **p1** point to the ninth element of **p1**'s type beyond the one it is currently pointing to.

Beyond addition and subtraction of a pointer and an integer, no other arithmetic operations may be performed on pointers: you may not multiply or divide pointers; you may not add or subtract two pointers; you may not apply the bitwise shift and mask operators to them; and you may not add or subtract type **float** or **double** to pointers.

Pointer Comparisons

Two pointers that refer to separate types of variables have no relationship to each other. For example, if **p1** and **p2** are pointers that point to two separate and unrelated variables, any comparison between **p1** and **p2** is meaningless because **p1** and **p2** are clearly unequal. However, if both **p1** and **p2** point to variables that are related to each other—such as elements of the same array—**p1** and **p2** may be meaningfully compared. Therefore, pointers having such a relationship may be used in relational and logical operations.

For example, imagine that you are constructing stack routines to hold integer values. A *stack* is a list that uses "first-in, last-out" accessing. (It is often compared to a stack of plates on a table because the first one set down is the last one to be used.) Stacks are used frequently in compilers, interpreters, spreadsheets, and other system-related software.

To create a stack, you would need two routines, **push( )** and **pop( )**, and some free memory area for your stack. You would first need to use the standard function **malloc( )** to acquire the memory area. A **malloc( )** returns a character pointer. If **p1** represents the stack pointer, then the following code will initialize it to the start of 50 bytes of free memory. For this example, assume that your machine uses two bytes for integers; this code will not be portable to every computer:

```
int *p1, *tos;
char *malloc();  /* declare malloc() to be returning
                     a character pointer */

p1 = malloc(50);
tos = p1;        /* let tos hold top of stack */
```

The variable **tos** will hold the memory address of the top of the stack and will be used to prevent stack underflows. After the stack has been initialized, **push( )** and **pop( )** may be used as a stack for integers, as shown here:

```
push(i)
int i;
{
        p1++;
        if(p1==(tos+25)) {
                printf("stack overflow");
                exit();
        }
        *p1=i;

}

pop()
{
        if((p1-1)==tos) {
                printf("stack underflow");
                exit();
        }
        p1--;
        return *(p1+1);
}
```

Both the **push( )** and **pop( )** functions perform a relational test on the pointer **p1** to detect limit errors. In **push( )**, **p1** is tested against the end of stack by adding 25 to **tos**. Remember that in this example, integers are assumed to be two bytes long. In **pop( )**, **p1** is checked against **tos** to be sure that a stack underflow has not occurred.

In **pop( )**, without the parentheses, the **return** statement would look like

```
return *p1+1;
```

which would return the value at location **p1** plus one, not the value of the location **p1+1**. You must be very careful to use parentheses to ensure the correct order of evaluation when using pointers.

This implementation will store only 24, not 25, values, leaving the first two bytes of memory unused. (Later you will rewrite it to store all 25.)

Pointers and Arrays

As you may have already guessed, there is a close relationship between pointers and arrays. For example, in

```
char str[80];
char *p1;

p1 = str;
```

p1 has been set to the address of the first array element in **str**. If you wished to access the fifth element in **str**, you could write

```
str[4]
```

or

```
*(p1+4)
```

Both statements will return the fifth element. Remember, since arrays start at zero, a four is used to index **str**. You would also add four to the pointer **p1** to get the fifth element because **p1** currently points to the first element of **str**.

In essence, C allows two methods of accessing array elements. This is important because pointer arithmetic can be *faster* than array indexing. Since speed is often a consideration in programming, the use of pointers to access array elements is very common in C programs.

For example, these are two versions of **puts( )**, —one with array indexing,

```
puts(s)   /* with arrays */
char *s;
{
        register int t;

        for(t=0;s[t];++t)
                putchar(s[t]);
}
```

and one with pointers,

```
put(s)   /* with pointers */
char *s;
{
        while(*s) putchar(*s++);
}
```

Most professional C programmers would find the second version easier to read and understand, so this is the way routines of this sort are commonly written in C.

Do not think that array indexing is wrong because it *does* have its place. Just remember that if the array is going to be accessed in strictly ascending or descending order, pointers are faster and easier to use. If the array is going to be accessed randomly, array indexing is probably a little better because it is easier to read and code, although pointers would still be faster.

Pointers to Character Arrays

Prior to this chapter, all operations on strings were performed by indexing the character array. However, most string operations in C are usually performed by pointers to the array and pointer arithmetic because pointers are faster and easier to use.

The following are two ways to write the function **strcmp( )**, which is found in the library of your C compiler:

```
strcmp(s1,s2)   /* with arrays */
char *s1, *s2;
{
        register int t;

        for(t=0;s1[t];++t)
                if(s1[t]!=s2[t]) return s1[t];
        if(s2[t]) return (s2[t]);
        return '\0'
}
```

and

```
strcmp(s1,s2)   /* with pointers */
char *s1, *s2;
{
        while(*s1)
                if(*s1++!=*s2++) return *(s1--);
        if(*s2) return (*s2);
        return '\0';
}
```

In case you have forgotten, all strings in C are terminated by a null, which is a false value. Therefore, a statement like

```
while (*s1)
```

is true until the end of the string is reached.

Most string functions will resemble the **strcmp( )** with pointers where loop control is concerned. It is faster, more efficient, and easier to understand than arrays.

In the **strcmp( )** function, both **s1** and **s2** were local variables. They could be altered with no side effects on the calling variables. However, be careful. Can you find the error in the program given in Figure 7-1?

In Figure 7-1, **p1** is assigned the address of **s** once. This assignment is outside the loop. During the first time through the loop, **p1** does point to the first character in **s**. However, during the second time through, it continues from where it left off because it was not reset to the start of the array **s**. This next character may be part of the second string, another variable, or another

```
main()    /* this program has a bug */
{
        char s[80];
        char *p1;

        p1=s;
        do {
                gets(s);            /* read a string */
                while(*p1) printf(" %d",*p++);
                /* print the decimal equivalent of each
                    character */
        } while(!strcmp(s,"done"));
}
```

Figure 7-1. A program with an error

piece of the program. Eventually, this will "crash" the program.

The proper way to write this program is given in Figure 7-2. Each time the loop iterates, **p1** is set to the start of the string. Remember, you must know where your pointers are pointing at all times.

```
main()    /* this program is correct */
{
        char s[80];
        char *p1;

        do {
                p1=s;
                gets(s);            /* read a string */
                while(*p1) printf(" %d",*p++);
                /* print the decimal equivalent of each
                    character */
        } while(!strcmp(s,"done"));
}
```

Figure 7-2. The correct version of the program in Figure 7-1

Arrays of Pointers

Pointers may be arrayed just like any other data type. The declaration for an **int** pointer array of size 10 is

```
int *x[10];
```

To assign the address of an integer variable called **var** to the third element of the pointer array, you would write

```
int var;

x[2]=&var;
```

Remember that you are working with an array of pointers. The only values that the array elements may hold are the addresses of integer variables. To find the value of **var**, you would write

```
*x[2]
```

If you want to pass an array of pointers into a function, you may use the same method used for other arrays—simply call the function with the array name without any indexing. For example, a function that will receive array **x**, which was declared earlier, would look like this:

```
func1(q)
int *q[];
{
        int t;

        t = *q[2];   /* gets value of integer pointed
                        to by the third pointer in q */
}
```

You must use the [ ] to signify an array. The **q** is not a pointer to integers, but rather a pointer to an array of pointers to integers. Never forget what kind of pointers you are dealing with.

A common use of pointer arrays is to hold pointers to error messages. You can create a function that will output a message based on the integer number of that message. For example, **serror( )** uses **init_messages( )** to initialize **err**, a character-pointer array that is global.

```
char *err[5];
init_messages()
{
        err[0]="syntax error";
        err[1]="parentheses expected";
        err[2]="undefined variable";
        err[3]="duplicate label name";
}

serror(i)        /* report errors based on i */
{
        printf(err[i]);
}
```

As you can see, **printf( )** inside **serror( )** is called with a character pointer, which points to one of the various error messages.

You should now see the similarity between this code and the way that command-line arguments are accessed. Remember, command-line arguments are contained in **argv**, an array of character pointers.

Pointers to Arrays in General

Pointers to any type of array operate as an alternative form of indexing. There are a few concepts that you should keep in mind when using pointers to arrays.

Comparisons between pointers that do not access the same array are invalid and *will* cause errors. You can never know where your data will be placed in memory, if it will be placed there in the same way again, or whether each compiler will treat it in the same way. Therefore, making any comparisons between pointers to two different arrays will yield unexpected results. For example,

```
char s[80];
char y[80];
char *p1, *p2;
p1=s;
p2=y;
if(p1 < p2)...
```

is intrinsically an invalid concept. Do not do this type of programming unless your application is very unusual and requires knowledge of the memory locations of certain variables.

A related error assumes that two back-to-back arrays may be indexed as one by simply incrementing a pointer across the array boundaries. For example, this code

```
int first[10];
int second[10];
int *p,t;
p=first;
for(t=0;t<20;++t)  *p++=t;
```

cannot be used to initialize arrays **first** and **second** with the numbers 0 through 19. Even though it may work on some compilers under certain circumstances, it assumes that both arrays will first be placed back to back in memory. It may not always be the case and usually, it can only lead to trouble.

Pointers To Pointers

When you were working with arrays of pointers, you were actually working with *pointers to pointers*. The concept of arrays of pointers is straightforward because the indexes keep the meaning clear. However, pointers to pointers can be very confusing.

A pointer to a pointer is a form of multiple indirection, or a chain of pointers. As you can see in Figure 7-3, in the case of a normal pointer, the value of the pointer is the address of the variable that contains the value desired. In the case of a pointer to a pointer, the first pointer contains the address of the second pointer, which points to the variable that contains the value desired.

Multiple indirection can be carried on to whatever extent desired, but there are few cases where more than a pointer to a pointer is needed—or even wise to use. Excessive multiple indirection is difficult to follow and prone to conceptual errors. (Do not confuse multiple indirection with the far simpler concept of *linked lists*, such as those used in databases.)

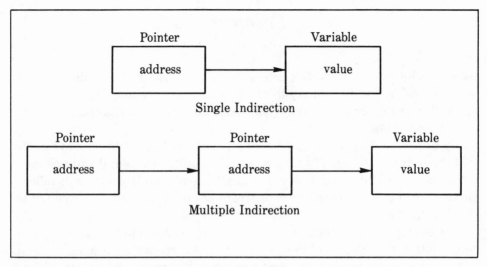

Figure 7-3. Single and multiple indirection

An example of how to use a pointer to a pointer is the short program given in Figure 7-4.

The program declares **p** as a pointer to an integer and **q** as a pointer to a pointer to an integer. The call to **printf( )** will print the number 10 on the screen. This is a contrived use of multiple indirection but serves to show the procedure clearly.

```
main()
{
        int x,*p,**q;

        x = 10;
        p = &x;
        q = &p;
        printf("%d", **q); /* print the value of x */
}
```

Figure 7-4. A program that shows the use of a pointer to a pointer

Initializing Pointers

After a pointer is declared but before it has been assigned, it will contain a nonsense value. Should you try to use the pointer prior to giving it a value, you will probably crash not only your program, but even the operating system of your computer.

By convention, a pointer may be initialized to null, usually zero, to signify that it points to nothing. The idea is that if a pointer has a null value, it does not point to anything and is free for use. This is a good practice to follow. However, you can still crash your program or operating system if you try to assign a null value to it.

For example, the **malloc( )** function, found in the standard library, will return either the address of the memory that you requested or a null. A null signifies that your memory request was denied because of the lack of free memory.

You can use the null pointer to make many of your pointer routines easier. In a function that searches an array of pointers, if you assume that the search can stop when a null pointer is found, you will not need to search the entire array. In this example,

```
search(p)
int *p[];
{
        register int t;

        for(t=0;t<array_size && p[t];++t)
                if(!p[t]) return t;
        return -1; /* not found */
}
```

search( ) assumes that the pointer array used in calling will contain either valid addresses or nulls. This presupposes that it was initialized elsewhere.

As with any variable, pointer arrays may be initialized when they are declared. If you recall the function **serror( )** from earlier in this chapter, the array **err**, which held pointers to the error messages, was explicitly initialized by a separate routine. The array **err** was also global. It is possible to eliminate the initialization function by making **err** a local **static** array. The following version of **serror( )** requires no initialization or global variables.

```
serror(i) /* better version */
int t;
{
        static char *err[] = {
                "syntax error",
                "parentheses expected",
                "undefined variable",
                "duplicate label name"
        };
        printf(err[i]);
}
```

The [ ] pair after **err** signifies to the compiler that it should count the elements and create an array large enough to hold them. This version can completely stand alone and does not reinitialize the array with each call.

Pointers To Functions

A particularly confusing yet powerful use of pointers is *pointers to functions*. Even though a function is not a variable, it still has a location in memory that can be assigned to a pointer. This pointer can then be used to manipulate function calls.

To understand what a pointer to a function means, you must understand a little about how a function is compiled and called in C. First, as each function is compiled, source code is transformed into object code, which performs the activities of the function. Second, at link time, the address where the function code begins is known. When a call is made to a function while your program is running, a machine language "call" is made to the memory address of the function. Therefore, a pointer to a function actually contains the memory address of the beginning of the function's code.

To understand the concept of a pointer to a function, consider the program in Figure 7-5, paying close attention to the declarations.

The **strcmp( )** is the standard string-comparing function found in the standard library. It is declared in **main( )** so that the program will know what type of value it is returning—in this case, an integer—and that it is a function, not a variable. When the function **check( )** is called, two character

```
        main()
        {
                int strcmp(); /* declare a function */
                char s1[80],s2[80];

                gets(s1);
                gets(s2);
                check(s1,s2,strcmp);
        }
        check(a,b,cmp)
        char *a,*b;
        int (*cmp) ();
        {
                printf("testing for equality\n");

                if(!(*cmp) (a,b)) printf("equal");
                else printf("not equal");
        }
```

Figure 7-5. A program that uses a pointer to a function

pointers and one function pointer are passed as parameters. Inside the function **check( )**, the arguments are declared as character pointers and a function pointer. You must use exactly the same method as shown in Figure 7-5 when declaring a function pointer. The parentheses are needed so the compiler can interpret this statement correctly. Without the parentheses around ***cmp**, the compiler would assume that you are simply declaring a function, which is not what is meant here.

Once inside **check( )**, you can see how the **strcmp( )** function is called. The statement

```
(*cmp) (a,b)
```

will perform a call to the function—in this case, **strcmp( )**, which **cmp** points to with the arguments **a** and **b**.

You may be asking yourself why anyone would want to write a program in this way. Obviously nothing is gained and significant confusion is introduced. However, there are times when it is advantageous to pass arbitrary functions into procedures or to keep an array of functions.

Although it is beyond the scope of this book to develop an example in detail, the following discussion may help illustrate a use of function pointers.

When a compiler is written, it is common for the part of it that evaluates arithmetic expressions to perform function calls to various support routines; for example, the sine, cosine, and tangent functions. Instead of having a large **switch** statement with all of these functions listed in them, an array of function pointers can be kept and an index generated directly. Once the index is known, the proper function can be called.

The function **check** in Figure 7-6 can be made to check for either alpha-

```
main()
{
        int strcmp(); /* declare a function */
        int numcmp();
        char s1[80],s2[80];

        gets(s1);
        gets(s2);
        printf("numeric (n) or alphabetic (a)? ");
        if(getchar()=='a')
                check(s1,s2,strcmp);
        else
                check(s1,s2,numcmp);
}

check(a,b,cmp)
char *a,*b;
int (*cmp) ();
{
        printf("testing for equality\n");

        if(!(*cmp) (a,b)) printf("equal");
        else printf("not equal");
}

numcmp(a,b)
char *a,*b;
{
        if(atoi(a)==atoi(b)) return 0;
        else return 1;
}
```

Figure 7-6. A program, which shows the use of function pointers

betical equality or numeric equality with a simple change. Either type of equality may be tested by a call to the same function.

You may never have the need to use pointers to functions. They exist because C replaces assembly language programming. In assembler it is possible to load an address register and perform a call to that address. Pointers to functions allow the same procedure.

Pointers Are Not Integers

Pointers are not integers—they are not unsigned integers either. For example, the short program in Figure 7-7 allocates a region of memory and assigns it to a character pointer.

Although the program looks fine and will generally compile and run without errors on all current microcomputers and C implementations, it is not *technically* correct. The reason is that the compiler will assume that **malloc( )** is returning an integer, when in fact it is returning a character pointer. Most of the time this will not cause problems, but to ensure portability, the program should be rewritten as shown in Figure 7-8.

The reason that pointers cannot be treated as integers in general is that some processors may perform certain sign adjustments on them, or that the size of an integer may not be the size of an address. Whatever the reason, it pays to be careful.

```
main()
{
        char *p;

        p = malloc(100); /* get 100 bytes */
}
```

Figure 7-7. A technically incorrect program that allocates a region of memory and assigns it to a character pointer

```
main()
{
        char *p, *malloc();

        p = malloc(100); /* get 100 bytes */
}
```

Figure 7-8. The corrected version of the program in Figure 7-7

Problems
With Pointers

Nothing will get you into more trouble than a "wild" pointer. Pointers are a mixed blessing. They give you tremendous power and are necessary for several systems programs, but when a pointer accidentally contains a wrong value, it can be the most difficult bug to track down.

An erroneous pointer bug is difficult to find because the pointer itself is not the problem; the problem is that each time you perform an operation using it, you are reading or writing to some unknown piece of memory. If you read from it, the worst that can happen is that you get garbage. However, if you write to it, you will be writing over other pieces of your code or data. This, in turn, may not show up until later in the execution of your program and may lead you to look for the bug in the wrong place. There may be little or no evidence to suggest that the pointer is the problem. This type of bug has caused programmers to lose sleep time and time again.

Because pointer errors are such nightmares, you should do your best never to generate one. To avoid pointer errors, you should see how to create them so you may never do it. The classic example of a pointer error is the *uninitialized pointer*, shown in Figure 7-9.

The **p** in Figure 7-9 contains an unknown address because it has never been defined. You will have no way of knowing where the value of **x** has been written. When your program is very small, as it is in this figure, the odds are that **p** will contain an address that is not in your code or data area. Most of

```
main()  /* this program is wrong */
{
        int x, *p;

        x = 10;
        *p = x;
}
```

Figure 7-9. An incorrect program that uses an uninitialized pointer

the time your program will appear to work fine. However, as your program grows, the probability of **p** having a pointer into either your program's code or data area *increases*. Eventually your program stops working. The solution is always to make sure that a pointer is pointing at something valid before it is used.

A second common error is caused by a simple misunderstanding of how to use a pointer. In Figure 7-10, the call to **printf( )** will not print the value of **x**, which is 10, onto the screen. It will print some unknown value because the assignment

```
p = x;
```

is wrong. This statement has assigned the value 10 to the pointer **p**, which

```
main()  /* this program is wrong */
{
        int x, *p;

        x = 10;
        p = x;
        printf("%d", *p);
}
```

Figure 7-10. A program that incorrectly uses a pointer

was supposed to contain an address, not a value. To correct the program, you should write

```
p = &x;
```

That pointers handled incorrectly can cause very tricky bugs is not a reason to avoid their use. You should simply be careful and make sure you know where each pointer is pointing before using it.

E X E R C I S E S

1. Let **x** be an integer and **p** be an integer pointer. Write the code fragment that will assign the value 10 to **x** using pointer **p1**.

2. Write a function called **swapg( )** that will exchange the value of two integers if, and only if, the first argument is greater than the second.

3. Rewrite the **push( )** and **pop( )** routines so that that all 25 elements may be used.

4. Using pointers instead of array indexes, rewrite **putw( )** from Chapter 6.

5. What is wrong with this function?
```
func1()
{
        char *p;
        char s[80];

        p = s[0];
        gets(s);
        printf("%s ",p);
}
```

6. Write a short function that will print the value of each element pointed to by an array of **float** pointers. Assume that the array is ten elements long.

A N S W E R S

```
1. p = &x;
   *p = 10;


2. swapg(a,b)
   int *a,*b;
   {
           register int t;

           if(*a<=*b) return; /* no swap */
           t = *a;
           *a = *b;
           *b = t;
   }


3. push(i)
   int i;
   {
           if(p1==(tos+25)) {
                   printf("stack overflow");
                   exit();
           }
           *p1=i;
           p1++;
   }

   pop()
   {
           if((p1)==tos) {
                   printf("stack underflow");
                   exit();
           }
           p1--;
           return *p1;
   }


4. putw(i,fp)
   int i;
   FILE *fp;
   {
           char *t;

           t=&i;   /* assign the address of i to char *t */
           putc(*t++,fp);
           putc(*t,fp);
   }
```

5. The **p** is assigned the value of the first element of array **s**, not its address. The intention was to assign the address of the first element in the array.

6.
```
func1(f)
float *f[];
{
        register int t;

        for(t=0;t<10;++t) printf("%f ",*f[t]);
}
```

Arrays

C H A P T E R   8

Previous chapters introduced single-dimensional arrays. In this chapter, several array topics will be covered, with an emphasis on multidimensional arrays.

In C all arrays consist of contiguous memory locations. The lowest address corresponds to the first element, and the largest address to the last element.

The general declaration for a single-dimensional array is

type var—name[dimension];

The declaration statement is similar to the **DIM** statement in BASIC. While some BASICs have a default length for arrays, C requires that each array be given a length in its declaration statement.

C arrays begin at zero. When you write

```
char p[10];
```

you are declaring a character array that has 10 array elements, p[0] through p[9]. The following examples in C and in BASIC illustrate this important point:

```
int x[10];  /* this reserves 10 integer elements */
int t;

for(t=0;t<10;++t) x[t]=t;
```

versus

```
10 DIM X(10)
20 FOR T=1 TO 10
30    X(T) = T
40 NEXT
```

The BASIC version indexes the array **X** from 1 through 10, whereas the C version indexes from 0 through 9. Although most BASICs will allow you to start arrays at 0, most BASIC programmers do not. If you are a BASIC programmer, starting at 0 will take a little getting used to. The crucial difference is that in BASIC, the number in the **DIM** statement generally specifies the last element, while in C the number in the declaration statement specifies the number of elements.

C has no bounds checking on arrays; you could overwrite either end of an array and write into some other variable's data or even into a piece of the program. In correctly written programs, this is generally not a problem, but it can be when you are learning to program in C. Therefore, be especially careful. For example, make certain that the character arrays that accept character input using **gets( )** are long enough to accept the longest input.

When you pass an array as a function argument, the address of the first element of the array is passed to the function. An entire copy of the array is not made. This means that any operations you perform on that array while inside a function will affect the array outside the function. In other words, you may alter array arguments to a function.

Single-Dimensional Arrays

Single-dimensional arrays are essentially lists of information of one type. The most common example of single-dimensional arrays is a character string. When declaring a character array to be used to hold a string, you must allow one extra byte for the null terminator, which all strings have. For example, if you wished to declare an array s for a 10-character string, you would write

```
char s[11];
```

This makes room for the null at the end of the string.

When passing single-dimensional arrays to functions, you call the function with the array name. For example, to pass array s to the function **gets( )**, you would write

```
gets(s);
```

This causes the address of the first element of s to be passed to **gets( )**. You are actually passing a character pointer.

If a function will be receiving a single-dimensional array, you may declare the formal parameter in one of two ways: as a pointer or as an array. For example, to receive s into a function called **func1( )**, you could declare **func1( )** as either

```
func1(str)
char *str;
{
  .
  .
  .
```

or

```
func1(str)
char str[ ];
{
  .
  .
  .
```

Both methods of declaration are identical because each tells the compiler that a character pointer is going to be received.

Actually, as far as the compiler is concerned,

```
func1(str)
char str[11];
{
  .
  .
  .
```

would also work because C will generate code that instructs **func1( )** to receive a character pointer. Since there is no bounds checking, an array of any size may be passed in the calling routine, even though only a size of 11 was declared.

Two-Dimensional Arrays

C allows multidimensional arrays. The simplest form of the multidimensional array is the two-dimensional array. A two-dimensional array is, in essence, an array of one-dimensional arrays. To declare a two-dimensional integer array **d** of size 10,20, you would write

```
int d[10][20];
```

Pay careful attention to the declaration: unlike most other computer languages, which use commas to separate the array dimensions, C places each dimension in its own brackets.

Similarly, to access point 3,5 of array **d**, you would use

```
d[3][5]
```

If you know BASIC, you will find the programs in Figure 8-1 useful. Both the BASIC and the C versions will load a two-dimensional array with the numbers 1 through 12.

In the C version, num[0][0] will have value 1, num[0][1] the value 2, num[0][2] the value 3, and so on. The value of num[2][3] will be 12.

Two-dimensional arrays are stored in a row-column matrix, where the first index indicates the row and the second index indicates the column. This means that the rightmost index changes faster than the leftmost when sequencing through the array. Figure 8-2 shows a two-dimensional array in memory. In essence, the first index can be thought of as a pointer to the correct row.

Remember that storage for all array elements is allocated permanently. In the case of a two-dimensional array, the following formula will find the number of bytes of memory:

bytes = row * column * number of bytes in data type

```
        main()
        {
                int t,i, num[3][4];

                for(t=0;t<3;++t)
                        for(i=0;i<4;++i)
                                num[t][i]=(t*4)+i+1;
        }

10 DIM N(3,4)
20 FOR T=1 TO 3
30     FOR I=1 TO 4
40         N(T,I)=((T-1)*4)+I
50     NEXT
60 NEXT
```

Figure 8-1. C and BASIC versions of a program that loads a two-dimensional array

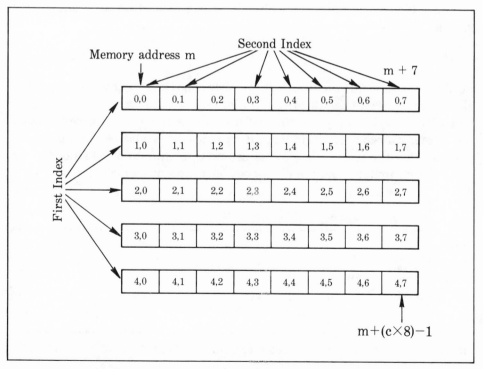

Figure 8-2. Two-dimensional array in memory

Therefore, an integer array with dimensions 10,5 would have $10 \times 5 \times 2$, or 100 bytes allocated. Remember that large arrays use lots of memory, so be careful that you only declare an array large enough for your purposes.

When passing two-dimensional arrays into functions, you pass only a pointer to the first element. You can do this by using the array name without indexes. However, a function receiving a two-dimensional array as a parameter must define the length of the second dimension. For example, a function that will receive a two-dimensional integer array with dimensions 10,10 would be declared like this:

```
func1(x)
int x[ ][10];
{

        .
        .
        .

}
```

It would be possible to give the first dimension as well, but it is not necessary.

C needs to know the second dimension in order to work on statements such as

```
x[2][4]
```

inside the function. If the length of the rows is not known, it would be impossible to know where the third row begins.

Figure 8-3 shows a program that uses a two-dimensional array to store the numeric grade for each student in a teacher's classes. The program assumes that the teacher has 3 classes and a maximum of 30 students per class. Work through this example to see how the array elements are accessed.

```
#define CLASSES 3
#define GRADES  30
int grade[CLASSES][GRADES];

main()  /* class grades program */
{
```

Figure 8-3. A program that uses a two-dimensional array to store numeric grades

```
            char ch;

            do {
              do {
                    printf("(E)nter grades\n");
                    printf("(R)eport grades\n");
                    printf("(Q)uit\n");
                    ch=toupper(getchar());
              } while(ch!='E' && ch!='R' && ch!='Q');
              switch(ch) {
                    case 'E':
                            enter_grades();
                            break;
                    case 'R':
                            disp_grades(grade);
                            break;
                    case 'Q':
                            exit(0);
              }
            } while(1);
}

enter_grades()
{
        int t,i;

        for(t=0;t<CLASSES;t++) {
                printf("Class # %d:\n",t+1);
                for(i=0;i<GRADES;++i) {
                        grade[t][i]=get_grade(i);
                }
        }
}

get_grade(num)
int num;
{
        char s[80];

        printf("enter grade for student # %d:\n",num+1);
        gets(s);
        return(atoi(s));
}

disp_grades(g)
int g[][CLASSES];
{
        int t,i;

        for(t=0;t<CLASSES;++t) {
                printf("Class # %d:\n",t+1);
                for(i=0;i<GRADES;++i) {
                        printf("grade for student #%d is %d\n",
                                i+1,g[t][i]);
                }
        }
}
```

Figure 8-3. A program that uses a two-dimensional array to store numeric grades (*continued*)

The function **disp—grades( )** was called with the array **grades** passed as an argument. Notice that the second dimension of the parameter **g** was explicitly specified, as is required when passing two-dimensional arrays.

Multidimensional Arrays

C allows arrays of greater than two dimensions. The exact limit, if any, will be determined by your compiler. The general form of a multidimensional array declaration is

type name[a][b][c]...[z];

Arrays of three or more dimensions are not often used because of the amount of memory required to hold them. As stated before, storage for all array elements is allocated permanently during the execution of your program. For example, a four-dimensional character array with dimensions 10,6,9,4 would require $10 \times 6 \times 9 \times 4$, or 2160 bytes. If the array were integer, 4320 bytes would be allocated. If the array were double float, then 34,560 bytes would be required. The required storage increases exponentially with the number of dimensions. The computer takes time to generate each index and this can cause multidimensional arrays to access slower than a single-dimensional array with the same number of elements. For these and other reasons, when large multidimensional arrays are needed, you should dynamically allocate bits and pieces of the array, as needed, and use pointers. However, this procedure, called *sparse-array processing*, is beyond the scope of this book.

When passing multidimensional arrays into functions, you must declare all but the first dimension. For example, if you declare array **m** as

```
int m[4][3][6][5];
```

then a function, **func1( )**, which will receive **m**, would look like

```
func1(d)
int d[ ][3][6][5];
{
.
.
.
```

Arrays Versus Pointers
In Multidimensional Arrays

In the last chapter you learned that pointers and single-dimensional arrays could easily be interchanged. This holds true for arrays of two or more dimensions. For example, consider this array:

```
char p[10];
```

The following statements are identical:

```
p
```

```
&p[0]
```

This statement

```
p==&p[0]
```

evaluates true because the address of the first element of an array is the same as the address of the array, which is derived by using its name without index.

When you consider character array **a**, which has two dimensions 10,10, you can see that these two statements are identical:

```
a
```

```
&a[0][0]
```

The 0,4 element may be referenced in two ways: either by the expected array indexing, **a[0][4]**, or by pointers, ***(a+4)**. Therefore, element 1,2 is either **a[1][2]** or ***(a+12)**. For a two-dimensional array, **a[j][k]** is equivalent to ***(a+(j*row length)+k)**.

In a sense, a two-dimensional array is like an array of row pointers and single-dimensional arrays of rows. Therefore, one easy way to use pointers to access two-dimensional arrays is by using a separate pointer variable. The reason you would want to use pointers instead of standard array indexing is for speed and efficiency. The following function will print the contents of the specified row for the global integer array **num**:

```
num[10][10]
pr_row(j)
int j;
{
        int *p,t;
```

```
        p = &num[j][0]; /* get address of first
                           element in row j */
        for(t=0;t<10;++t) printf("%d ",*(p+t));
}
```

The loop that prints the elements of the row will run much faster using pointer arithmetic than it will using array indexes. The reason is that pointers are incremented with a simple set of machine instructions, but indexing an array requires a series of computations, which takes longer.

This routine can be made completely general by making the calling arguments the row, the row length, and a pointer to the first array element, as shown here:

```
pr_row(j,row_dimension, p) /* general */
int j,row_dimension;
int *p;
{
        int t;

        p = p + (j * row_dimension);
        for(t=0;t<row_dimension;++t)
                printf("%d ",*(p+t));
}
```

Arrays of greater than two dimensions may be thought of in the same way. For example, a three-dimensional array can be reduced to a pointer to a two-dimensional array, which can be reduced to a pointer to a one-dimensional array.

Generally, an n-dimensional array can be reduced to a pointer and an $n-1$ dimensional array. This new array can be reduced again using the same method. The process ends when a single-dimensional array is produced.

Allocated Arrays

In C you can dynamically allocate and free memory by using the standard library routines **malloc( )** and **free( )**. (In some implementations **alloc( )** is the allocation function.) If memory is limited and you need an array for only a short time, you could allocate it by using **malloc( )** and return it to free memory by using **free( )** when you are done.

This fragment allocates 1000 bytes of memory.

```
char *p;

p = malloc(1000); /* get 1000 bytes */
```

The **p** points to the first of 1000 bytes of free memory. If you needed to utilize that memory as a two-dimensional array of dimensions 10,10 to perform the array processing, you could declare a function similar to this one:

```
process(s)
char s[][10];
{
/* process array */
}
```

This tricks the C compiler by simulating a 10-by-10-character array. Actually, you do have a 10-by-10-character array inside the function; the difference is that you performed the allocation manually by using the **malloc( )** statement, rather than automatically by using the normal array-declaration statement.

The essential sequence of allocation, processing, and de-allocation are shown in the following program abstract. This will allocate memory for a 10-by-10-character array, pass the pointer to that memory into a function called **process( )**, and free the memory when process returns:

```
main( )
{
    char *p;
    .
    .
    .
    p = malloc(1000);
    process(p);
    free(p);
    .
    .
    .
}
process(ax)
char ax[10][10];
{
    .
    .
    .
    /* ax may be used as a normal two-
    dimensional character array */
    .
    .
    .
}
```

Because coding of this nature can be misleading and confusing to someone reading your program, you should only do this when memory is in short supply. It is better style, when possible, to declare arrays explicitly. However, the use of **malloc( )**, **free( )**, and dynamic allocation in general is certainly acceptable.

A Longer Example

Two-dimensional arrays are commonly used to simulate board game matrices like chess and checkers. While it is beyond the scope of this book to present a chess or checkers program, look at Figure 8-4, which lists a program that plays a poor game of tic-tac-toe. The tic-tac-toe matrix will be represented using a 3-by-3-character array.

The computer plays a very simple game. You are always **X** and the computer is **O**. When it is the computer's turn to move, it just scans the matrix and puts its **O** in the first empty location. If it cannot find an empty location, it reports a draw game and exits.

To simplify both the main loop and the matrix display routine, it is assumed that the **check( )** routine will return a space if there is no winner yet. The **check( )** will return an **X** if you have won or an **O** if the computer has won. To support this, the matrix must be initialized to contain spaces.

The routine **get_player_move( )** is recursive if an invalid location is entered. The program in Figure 8-4 is an example in which recursion can be used to simplify a routine and reduce code.

The **disp_matrix( )** function displays the current state of the game. You should be able to see how initializing the matrix with spaces simplified this function.

The **check( )** checks the matrix after each move to see if there is a winner. It scans the rows, the columns, and then the diagonals. You can see now how the program was simplified by using a space to denote no winner. Early in the game, this routine will return a space quickly because the matrix is full of spaces.

All the routines in this example access the array **matrix** different ways. Study them to make sure that you understand the array operation.

```
#define SPACE   ' '
char matrix[3][3];   /* the tic tac toe matrix */

main()
{
        char done;

        printf("This is the game of Tic Tac Toe.\n");
        printf("You will be playing against the computer.\n");
        done=SPACE;
        init_matrix();
        do {
                disp_matrix();
                get_player_move();
                done=check(); /* see if winner */
                if(done!=SPACE) break; /* winner!*/
                get_computer_move();
                done=check(); /* see if winner */
        } while(done==SPACE);
        if(done=='X') printf("You won!\n");
        else printf("I won!!!!\n");
        disp_matrix(); /* show final positions */
}

init_matrix()
{
        register int t;
        char *p;

        p = matrix;
        for(t=0;t<9;++t) *(p+t)=SPACE;
}

get_player_move()
{
        int x,y;

        printf("Enter coordinates for your X: ");
        scanf("%d%d",&x,&y);
        x--; y--;
        if(matrix[x][y]!=SPACE) {
                printf("Invalid move, try again.\n");
                get_player_move();
        }
        else matrix[x][y]='X';
}

get_computer_move()
{
        register int t;
        char *p;

        p = matrix;
        for(t=0;*p!=SPACE && t<9;++t) p++;
        if(t==9)  {
                printf("draw\n");
                exit(0); /* game over */
        }
        else *p='0';
```

Figure 8-4. A program that plays tic-tac-toe

```
        }

disp_matrix()
{
        int t,i;

        for(t=0;t<3;t++) {
                printf(" %c | %c | %c ",matrix[t][0],
                        matrix[t][1], matrix [t][2]);
                if(t!=2) printf("\n---|---|---\n");
        }
        printf("\n");
}

check()
{
        int t;
        char *p;

        for(t=0;t<3;t++) { /* check rows */
                p=&matrix[t][0];

                if(*p==*(p+1) && *(p+1)==*(p+2)) return *p;
        }

        for(t=0;t<3;t++) { /* check columns */
                p=&matrix[0][t];

                if(*p==*(p+3) && *(p+3)==*(p+6)) return *p;
        }

        /* test diagonals */
        if(matrix[0][0]==matrix[1][1] && matrix[1][1]==matrix[2][2])
                return matrix[0][0];
        if(matrix[0][2]==matrix[1][1] && matrix[1][1]==matrix[2][0])
                return matrix[0][2];
        return SPACE;
}
```

Figure 8-4. A program that plays tic-tac-toe (*continued*)

E X E R C I S E S

1. Write a function called **load( )** that loads in two ways a 10-byte character array called **a** with the letters a through j. The first way is using array indexing; the second is using pointers.

2. Write the declaration portion of a function called **func( )** that will receive the array **num**, which is declared here.

```
int num[100][1234];
```

3. Given

```
char str[10][5][3];
```

write a pointer expression that will return the value of **str[2][4][1]**.

4. How many bytes of memory will the following arrays need? Assume that integers are 2 bytes and floats are 8 bytes.

   a. `char s[80];`
   b. `char s[80][10];`
   c. `int n[10];`
   d. `float f[10][5];`
   e. `char x[10][9][8][7];`

5. What is wrong with the following abstract?

```
f(x)
int s[10][4][ ];
{
int t;
t = s[3][2][4];
.

.

.
}
```

6. Improve the tic-tac-toe program to play a better game.

7. Just for fun, rewrite the tic-tac-toe game to play against itself. Try to make each game different.

A N S W E R S

1.
```
load()
{
        int t;
        for(t=0;t<10;++t)  a[t]='a'+t;
}

load()
{
        int t;
        char *p;
        p=a;
        for(t=0;t<10;++t)  *p++='a'+t;
}
```

2.
```
func(n)
int n[][1234];
{
```

3. `*(str+(2*15)+(5*3)+3)`

4. *a.* 80 *b.* 800 *c.* 20 *d.* 400 *e.* 5040

5. The rightmost array dimension is missing. This dimension is necessary to the function to properly handle array indexing.

Structures, Unions, And User-defined Types

CHAPTER 9

C allows you to create new data types in two ways: first, by combining many variables into one conglomerate variable called a *structure;* and second, by using a *union* to allow many variables to share the same memory. You also can create new names for standard variable types using **typedef**. These features combine to give C a very rich set of variable types available to the programmer.

Structures

A *structure* is a collection of variables that is referenced under one name. Unlike BASIC, which has no way to link variables together, C uses structures to provide a convenient means of keeping related information in one place.

A *structure definition* forms a template that may be used to create structure variables. Each structure is made up of one or more variables that are logically related. These variables are called *structure elements*.

Structures, as logically connected groups of variables, can be passed easily to functions. Using structures can also make your source code much easier to read because the logical connection between structure elements is obvious.

For example, a name and address grouping in a mailing list is a common set of related information. The following code fragment declares a structure to hold the name and address fields; the keyword **struct** tells the compiler that a structure template is being defined:

```
struct addr {
        char name[30];
        char street[40];
        char city[20];
        char state[2];
        unsigned long int zip;
};
```

There are two aspects about this definition. First, it is terminated by a semicolon *because a structure definition is a statement.* Second, the structure tag **addr** identifies this particular data structure and is its name.

At this point *no variable has actually been declared.* Only the form of the data has been defined. To declare an actual variable with this structure, you would write

```
struct addr ainfo;
```

This will declare a variable of type *addr* called *ainfo*. When you define a structure, you are in essence defining a complex variable type made up of structure elements.

You may also declare one or more variables at the same time that you define a structure. For example,

```
struct addr {
        char name[30];
        char street[40];
        char city[20];
        char state[2];
        unsigned long int zip;
} ainfo, binfo, cinfo;
```

will define a structure called **addr** and declare variables **ainfo**, **binfo**, and **cinfo** of type **addr**.

If you only need one structure variable, the structure name is not needed. That means that

```
struct   {
         char name[30];
         char street[40];
         char city[20];
         char state[2];
         unsigned long int zip;
} ainfo;
```

declares one, called **ainfo**, variable of the structure preceding it.

The general form of a structure definition is

```
struct structure_name {
    type variable_name;
    type variable_name;
    type variable_name;
            .
            .
            .
} structure_variables;
```

where either the structure_name or the structure_variables may be omitted.

Referencing Structure Elements

The following code will assign the ZIP code 12345 to the structure variable **ainfo** declared earlier.

```
ainfo.zip = 12345;
```

As you can see, the structure variable name **ainfo** followed by a period and the element name will reference that individual structure element. The period is often called the *dot operator* by C programmers, but it essentially signifies that a *structure element* follows. All structure elements are accessed in the same way. The general form is

```
structure_name.element_name
```

Therefore, to print the ZIP code to the screen, you could write

```
printf("%d",ainof.zip);
```

This will print the ZIP code contained in the variable **zip** of the structure variable **ainfo**.

For example, consider **ainfo.name**. This element is an array of characters. Using **gets( )** to input a name, you would write

```
gets(ainfo.name);
```

This will pass a character pointer to the start of **name**.

If you wished to access the individual elements of **ainfo.name**, you could index **name**. For example, you could print the contents of **ainfo.name** by using

```
register int t;

for(t=0; ainfo.name[t]; ++t) putchar(ainfo.name[t]);
```

Arrays of Structures

Perhaps the most common usage of structures is in *arrays of structures*. To declare an array of structures, you must first define a structure and then declare an array variable of that type. For example, to declare a 100-element array of structures of type **addr** that had been defined earlier in the chapter, you would write

```
struct addr ainfo[100];
```

This creates 100 sets of variables that are organized as defined in the structure **addr**.

To print the ZIP code of structure 3, you would write

```
printf("%d",ainfo[2].zip);
```

Like all array variables, arrays of structures begin their indexing at zero.

A Mailing List Example

In this section, a simple Mailing List Program will be developed that uses an array of structures to hold the street address information. The functions in this program interact with structures and their elements to illustrate structure usage.

In this example, the information that will be stored includes

- name

- street

- city

- state

- ZIP code

To define the basic data structure, **addr**, that will hold this information, you would write

```
struct addr {
        char name[30];
        char street[40];
        char city[20];
        char state[3];
        unsigned long int zip;
};
```

Notice that the ZIP code field is an unsigned long integer. This is done because ZIP codes greater than 64000—such as 94564—cannot be represented in a two-byte integer. In this example, an integer is used to hold the ZIP code to illustrate a numeric structure element; however, the more common practice is to use a character string that accommodates ZIP codes with letters, as well as numbers.

Once the data structure has been defined, you can declare an array of structures with the following statement:

```
struct addr ainfo[100];
```

This declares an array called **ainfo**, which contains 100 structures of type **addr**.

The first function needed for the program is **main( )**:

```
main()   /* simple mailing list example using structures */
{
        char s[80], choice;

        init_list(); /* initialize the structure array*/
```

```
do {
    choice=menu_select();
    switch(choice) {
        case 1: enter();
                break;
        case 2: delete();
                break;
        case 3: list();
                break;
        case 4: exit(0);
    }
} while(1);

}
```

Here the function **init—list( )** prepares the structure array for use by putting a null character into the first byte of the name field. The program assumes that if the name field is empty, that structure variable is not in use. The **init—list( )** function is written as

```
init_list()
{
        register int t;

        for(t=0;t<100;++t) ainfo[t].name[0]='\0';
}
```

Next the **menu—select( )** function will display the option messages and return the user's selection:

```
menu_select()
{
        char s[80];
        int c;

        printf("1. Enter a name\n");
        printf("2. Delete a name\n");
        printf("3. List the file\n");
        printf("4. Quit\n");
        do {
                printf("\nEnter your choice: ");
                gets(s);
                c=atoi(s);
        } while(c<0 || c>4);
        return c;
}
```

The **enter( )** function prompts the user for input and places the information entered into the next free structure. If the array is full, the message **list**

full is printed on the screen. The **find_free( )** function searches the structure array for an unused element. Both functions are written as

```
enter()
{
        int slot;

        slot=find_free();
        if(slot==-1) {
                printf("\nlist full");
                return;
        }
        printf("enter name: ");
        gets(ainfo[slot].name);
        printf("enter street: ");
        gets(ainfo[slot].street);
        printf("enter city: ");
        gets(ainfo[slot].city);
        printf("enter state: ");
        gets(ainfo[slot].state);
        printf("enter zip: ");
        scanf("%d",&ainfo[slot].zip);
}
find_free()
{
        register int t;

        for(t=0;ainfo[t].name[0] && t<100;++t) ;
        if(t==100) return -1; /* no slots free */
        return t;
}
```

Notice that **find_free( )** returns a −1 if every structure array variable is in use. This is a safe number to use because there cannot be a −1 element.

The **delete( )** function simply requires the user to specify the number of the street address that needs to be deleted. The function then puts a null character in the first character position of the **name** field.

```
delete()
{
        register int slot;
        char s[80];

        printf("enter record #: ");
        gets(s);
        slot=atoi(s);
        if(slot>0 && slot < 100) ainfo[slot].name[0]='\0';
}
```

The final function the program needs is **list( )**, which prints the entire mailing list on the screen:

```
list()
{
        register int t;

        for(t=0;t<100;++t) {
                if(ainfo[t].name[0]) {
                        printf("%s\n",ainfo[t].name);
                        printf("%s\n",ainfo[t].street);
                        printf("%s\n",ainfo[t].city);
                        printf("%s\n",ainfo[t].state);
                        printf("%u\n",ainfo[t].zip);
                }
        }
        printf("\n\n");
}
```

Figure 9-1 gives the complete listing for the Mailing List Program. Compile and study the program so that you completely understand the structure references.

```
main()   /* simple mailing list example using structures */
{
        char s[80], choice;

        init_list(); /* initialize the structure array*/
        do {
             choice=menu_select();
             switch(choice) {
                  case 1: enter();
                          break;
                  case 2: delete();
                          break;
                  case 3: list();
                          break;
                  case 4: exit(0);
             }
        } while(1);

}
```

Figure 9-1. A simple Mailing List Program

```
init_list()
{
        register int t;
        for(t=0;t<100;++t) ainfo[t].name[0]='\0';
}

menu_select()
{
        char s[80];
        int c;

        printf("1. Enter a name\n");
        printf("2. Delete a name\n");
        printf("3. List the file\n");
        printf("4. Quit\n");
        do {
                printf("\nEnter your choice: ");
                gets(s);
                c=atoi(s);
        } while(c<0 || c>4);
        return c;
}

enter()
{
        int slot;

        slot=find_free();
        if(slot==-1) {
                printf("\nlist full");
                return;
        }
        printf("enter name: ");
        gets(ainfo[slot].name);
        printf("enter street: ");
        gets(ainfo[slot].street);
        printf("enter city: ");
        gets(ainfo[slot].city);
        printf("enter state: ");
        gets(ainfo[slot].state);
        printf("enter zip: ");
        scanf("%d",&ainfo[slot].zip);
}

find_free()
{
        register int t;
```

Figure 9-1. A simple Mailing List Program (*continued*)

```
            for(t=0;ainfo[t].name[0] && t<100;++t) ;
            if(t==100) return -1; /* no slots free */
            return t;
    }

delete()
{
        register int slot;
        char s[80];

        printf("enter record #: ");
        gets(s);
        slot=atoi(s);
        if(slot>0 && slot < 100) ainfo[slot].name[0]='\0';
    }

list()
{
        register int t;

        for(t=0;t<100;++t) {
                if(ainfo[t].name[0]) {
                        printf("%s\n",ainfo[t].name);
                        printf("%s\n",ainfo[t].street);
                        printf("%s\n",ainfo[t].city);
                        printf("%s\n",ainfo[t].state);
                        printf("%u\n",ainfo[t].zip);
                }
        }
        printf("\n\n");
    }
```

Figure 9-1. A simple Mailing List Program (*continued*)

Passing
Structures to Functions

Thus far all structures and arrays of structures used in the examples have been global. You will now learn how to pass a structure element to a function. When a structure is passed to a function, several changes occur in the way a structure element is referenced.

Passing Structure Elements to Functions

When you pass an element of a structure variable to a function, you are actually passing the value of that element to the function. Therefore, you are passing a simple variable. (Unless, of course, that element is complex, such as an array of characters.) For example,

```
struct fred {
        char x;
        int y;
        float z;
        char s[10];
} mike;
```

Here are examples of each element being passed to a function:

```
func(mike.x);  /* passes character value of x */
func2(mike.y); /* passes integer value of y */
func3(mike.z); /* passes float value of z */
func4(mike.s); /* passes address of string s */
func(mike.s[2]); /* passes character value of s[2] */
```

However, if you wished to pass the address of individual structure elements, you would place the **&** operator before the structure name. For example, to pass the address of the elements in the structure **mike**, you would write

```
func(&mike.x);  /* passes address of character x */
func2(&mike.y); /* passes address of integer y */
func3(&mike.z); /* passes address of float z*/
func4(mike.s); /* passes address of string s */
func(&mike.s[2]); /* passes address of character s[2] */
```

Notice that the **&** operator precedes the structure name, not the individual element name.

Passing Entire Structures to Functions

When a structure is passed to a function, only the address of the first byte of the structure is passed. This is similar to the way arrays are passed to functions. It is not feasible to copy the entire structure each time it is passed to a function; therefore, only its address is transferred. Because the function will be referencing the actual structure and not a copy, you will be able to modify the contents of the actual elements of the structure used in the call.

The general concept behind passing a structure to a function is that an address is passed. This means that you will be working with a *pointer* to a structure similar to the way you work with a pointer to an array. For example, Figure 9-2 gives a simple program that prints hours, minutes, and seconds on your screen. The actual timing of this program is adjusted by varying the loop count in **delay( )**.

As you can see in Figure 9-2, a global structure called **tm** was defined, but no variable was declared. Inside **main( )**, the structure **time** was declared and initialized to 0:0:0. This means that **time** is known directly only to the **main( )** function.

The two functions **update( )**, which changes the time, and **display( )**, which prints the time, are passed the address of **time**. In both functions, you can see that the argument is declared to be of structure type **tm**. This is necessary so that the compiler will know how to reference the structure elements.

The actual referencing is done by using pointers. For example, if you wanted to set the hours back to zero, you would write

```
if((*t).hours==24) (*t).hours=0;
```

This line of code tells the compiler to take the address of **t**, which is **time** in **main( )**, and assign zero to its element called **hours**. The parentheses are necessary around the *t because the dot operator has a higher priority than the *.

In actual practice, however, you will seldom, if ever, see references to a structure passed to a function as in the example just given. The reason is that this type of structure-element accessing is so common that a special operator is defined by C to perform this task. It is the ->. Most C programmers call this the *arrow operator*. It is formed by using the minus sign followed by a greater-than sign. The -> is used in place of the dot operator when accessing a structure element inside a function. For example,

```
(*t).hours
```

is the same as

```
t->hours
```

```
        struct tm {
                int hours;

                int minutes;
                int seconds;
        } ;

        main()   /* version 1 - explicit pointer references */
        {
                struct tm time;
                time.hours=0;
                time.minutes=0;
                time.seconds=0;
                do {
                        update(&time);
                        display(&time);
                } while(1);
        }

        update(t)
        struct tm *t;
        {
                (*t).seconds++;
                if((*t).seconds==60) {
                        (*t).seconds=0;
                        (*t).minutes++;
                }
                if((*t).minutes==60) {
                        (*t).minutes=0;
                        (*t).hours++;
                }
                if((*t).hours==24) (*t).hours=0;
                delay();
        }

        display(t)
        struct tm *t;
        {
                printf("%d:",(*t).hours);
                printf("%d:",(*t).minutes);
                printf("%d\n",(*t).seconds);
        }

        delay()
        {
                int t;
                for(t=1;t<1000;++t) ;
        }
```

Figure 9-2. A program that prints hours, minutes, and seconds on screen

Therefore, **update( )** could be rewritten as

```
update(t)
struct tm *t;
{
        t->seconds++;
        if(t->seconds==60) {
                t->seconds=0;
                t->minutes++;
        }
        if(t->minutes==60) {
                t->minutes=0;
                t->hours++;
        }
        if(t->hours==24) t->hours=0;
        delay();
}
```

You use the dot operator to access structure elements when the structure is either global or defined inside the same function as the code referencing it. You use the $->$ to reference structure elements when a structure pointer has been passed to a function.

Also remember that you have to pass the address of the structure to a function using the **&** operator. Structures are *not* like arrays, which can be passed by the array name only.

Arrays and Structures Within Structures

A structure element may be either simple or complex. A simple element is any of the built-in data types, such as integer or character. You have already seen one complex element: the character array used in **ainfo**. Other complex data types are single- and multidimensional arrays of the other data types and structures.

A structure element that is an array is treated as you might expect from the earlier examples. For example, in this listing

```
struct x {
        int a[10][10]; /* 10 x 10 array of ints */
        float b;
} y;
```

to reference integer 3,7 in **a** of structure **y**, you would write

```
y.a[3][7]
```

A structure can be an element of another structure, as in

```
struct ralph {
    struct addr newaddr[2]; /* array of structs of type x */
    char ch;
} tom;
```

where **addr** is the structure defined previously. Here a structure **ralph** has been defined as having two elements. The first element is an array of structures of type **addr**; the second is a character, **ch**. This code fragment will assign the ZIP code 61853 to the second element of **newaddr**:

```
tom. new addr[1]. zip = 61853
```

Bit Fields

Unlike most other computer languages, C has a built-in method to access a single bit within a byte. This can be useful for a number of reasons: first, if storage is limited, you can store several *Boolean* (true/false) variables in one byte; second, certain device interfaces transmit information encoded into bits within one byte; and third, certain encryption routines need to access the bits within a byte. Although all of these functions can be performed using bytes and the bitwise operators, a bit field can add more structure to your code and make it more portable.

The method C uses to access bits is based on the structure. This structure defines three variables of one bit each:

```
struct device {
        unsigned active : 1;
        unsigned ready : 1;
        unsigned xmt_error : 1;
} dev_code;
```

All three variables are declared as **unsigned** because a bit cannot have a sign. In fact, the only values a bit can have are 0 and 1. The structure variable **dev__code** might be used to decode information from the port of a tape drive, for example. The following code fragment will write a byte of information to the tape and check for errors using **dev—code**:

```
wr_tape(c)
char c;
{
        while(!dev_code.ready) rd(&dev_code); /* wait */
        wr_to_tape(c); /* write out byte */
        while(dev_code.active) rd(&dev_code); /* wait till
                                     info is written */
        if(dev_code.xmt_error) printf("write error");
}
```

Here, **rd( )** will return the status of the tape drive and **wr—to—tape( )** actually writes the data. Figure 9-3 shows what the bit-field variable **dev—code** looks like in memory.

As you can see from the previous example, each bit field is accessed using the structure dot operator. However, if the structure is passed to a function, you must use the —> operator.

You do not have to name each bit field. This makes it easy to pad up to the bit you want. For example, if the tape drive also returned an end-of-tape flag in bit 5, you could alter structure **device** to accommodate this using

```
struct device {
        unsigned active : 1;
        unsigned ready : 1;
        unsigned xmt_error : 1;
        unsigned : 1;
        unsigned : 1;
        unsigned EOT : 1;
} dev_code;
```

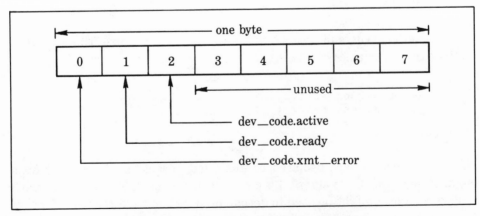

Figure 9-3. The bit-field variable **dev—code in memory**

Bit-field variables have certain restrictions. You cannot take the address of a bit-field variable. Bit-field variables cannot be arrayed. You cannot overlap integer boundaries. You cannot know, from machine to machine, whether the fields will run from right to left or from left to right; this implies that any code that uses bit fields may have some machine dependencies.

Using a union

In C a **union** is a memory location that is used by several different variables of potentially different types. Here is the definition of a **union**, called **u**, of a character and an integer:

```
union u {
        int i;
        char ch;
} ;
```

As with structures, this definition does not declare any variables. You may declare a variable either by placing its name at the end of the definition or by using a separate declaration statement. To declare a **union** variable **cnvt** of type **u** using the definition just given, you would write

```
union u cnvt;
```

In **union cnvt**, both integer **i** and character **ch** share the same memory location. (Of course, **i** occupies two bytes and **ch** uses only one.) Figure 9-4 shows how **i** and **ch** share the same address.

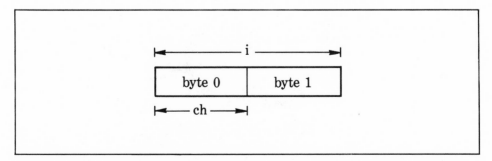

Figure 9-4. The memory location stored by integer **i** and character **ch**

When a **union** is declared, the compiler will automatically create a variable large enough to hold the largest variable type in the **union**.

To access a **union** element, you use the same syntax that you would use for structures: the dot and arrow operators. If the **union** variable is global, you use the dot operator; if the **union** variable is passed to a function, you use the arrow operator. For example, if **union cnvt** is global, to assign the integer 10 to its element **i**, you would write

```
cnvt.i=10;
```

However, if **cnvt** were passed to a function, you must use the −> operator:

```
func1(un)
union u un;
{
        un->i=10; /* assign 10 to cnvt using
                     function */
}
```

Using a **union** can aid in the production of machine-independent, or portable, code. Because the compiler keeps track of all sizes, no machine dependencies are produced. You need not worry about the size of an integer, character, or **float**. For example, you can use a **union** in type conversions. The **putw( )** function discussed in previous chapters will write the binary representation of an integer to a disk file. You have already seen two ways to write that function: the first with arrays and the second with pointers. Both methods use the fact that any address *can* be assigned to a pointer variable. Another perhaps more elegant way is by using a **union**. First you must create a **union** with one integer and a two-byte character array:

```
union pw {
        int i;
        char ch[2];
};
```

Now, **putw( )** can be written using this **union**:

```
putw(word,fp)    /* putw with union */
union pw word;
FILE *fp;
{
        putc(word->ch[0]);
        putc(word->ch[1]);
}
```

To write a word to a disk file, you would call **putw( )** with the integer value you wanted to write.

Using sizeof

You have seen that both structures and **union**s can be used to create variables of large sizes and that the actual size of these variables may change from machine to machine. The **sizeof** unary operator can be used to tell you the size of any variable type, including structures, **union**s, and user-defined variables. This can help eliminate machine-dependent code from your programs.

For example, these are the sizes of the data types for a C implementation that is common to many microcomputer C compilers:

type	size in bytes
char	1
int	2
long int	4
float	8
double	16

Therefore, this listing

```
char ch;
int i;
float f;

printf("%d",sizeof(ch));
printf("%d",sizeof(i));
printf("%d",sizeof(f));
```

will print the numbers 1, 2, and 8 on the screen.

The **sizeof** is a *compile-time operator*: all of the information necessary to compute the size of any variable is known at compile time. For example, consider the following code:

```
union x {
     char ch;
     int i;
     float f;
} tom;
```

The **sizeof(tom)** will be 8. At run time, it does not matter what the **union tom** is *actually* holding; all that matters is the size of the largest variable it can hold because the **union** must be as large as its largest element.

Using typedef

C allows you to define new data type names explicitly using the **typedef** keyword. You are not actually *creating* a new data class, but rather defining a new name for a type of data. This process can help make machine-dependent programs more portable; only the **typedef** statements would have to be changed. It also can aid in self-documenting your code by allowing descriptive names for the standard data types. The general form of the **typedef** statement is

```
typedef type name;
```

where **type** is any allowable data type and **name** is the new name for this type. The new name you define is in addition to—not a replacement for—the existing type name.

For example, you could create a new name for **float** using

```
typedef float balance;
```

This statement tells the compiler to recognize **balance** as another name for **float**. Next you could create a **float** variable using **balance**:

```
balance over_due;
```

Here, **over_due** is a floating-point variable of type **balance**, which is another word for **float**.

You can use **typedef** to create names for more complex types, too; for example,

```
typedef struct client {
        float due;
        int over_due;
        char name[40];
};
client clist[NUM_CLIENTS]; /* define array of
                            structures of type client */
```

Using **typedef** can help make your code easier to read and easier to port to a new machine. But remember—you are *not* creating any new data types.

E X E R C I S E S

1. Define a structure called **player** that will be able to store the following information:

       player name
       team name
       batting average

2. Using **player** from the previous exercise, declare a 100-element array of structures. Call this array **p_info**.

3. Write a short function called **enter( )** that will input the player's name, team name, and batting average from the keyboard. Your function will have the array index as its single argument. Assume that **p_info** is global.

4. Rewrite **enter( )** from the previous exercise assuming that **p_info** is passed to the function along with array index.

5. Write a structure called **crypt** that has the following bit-field variables:

       bit 0: **first**
       bit 1: **second**
       bit 4: **check_bit**

6. Define a **union** of the following variables:

       int i[4];
       char ch[8];
       float f;

7. What is wrong with this code?

```
if(sizeof(u)==2) printf("u has an integer in it");
else printf("u has a character in it");
```

8. Write the **typedef** statement that will make the name **width** the same as **float**.

A N S W E R S

```
1. struct player {
          char player_name[40];
          char player_team[40];
          float batting_average;
   };


2. struct player p_info[100];


3. enter(rec)
   int rec;
   {
          printf("enter player's name:");
          gets(p_info[rec].player_name);
          printf("enter player's team:");
          gets(p_info[rec].player_team);
          printf("enter player's batting average:");
          scanf("%f",p_info.batting_average);
   }


4. enter(rec,pi)
   int rec;
   struct player pi;
   {
          printf("enter player's name:");
          gets(p_info[rec]->player_name);
          printf("enter player's team:");
          gets(p_info[rec]->player_team);
          printf("enter player's batting average:");
          scanf("%f",p_info->batting_average);
   }


5. struct crypt {
          unsigned first : 1;
          unsigned second : 1;
          unsigned : 2;
          unsigned check_bit : 1;
   };
```

```
6. union u {
           int i;
           char ch;
           float f;
   };
```

7. The **sizeof** is a compile-time operator and has nothing to do with knowing what type of variable is actually stored somewhere.

```
8. typedef float width;
```

Writing a
C Program
CHAPTER 10

In this chapter, we will develop a more complex Mailing List Program that emphasizes design procedures and style and illustrates much of the C language. This example will show you the various steps of writing a successful C program.

There are three general approaches to writing a program: *top-down*, *bottom-up*, and *ad hoc*. In the *top-down* approach, you start with the top-level routine and move down to the low-level routines. The *bottom-up* approach works in the opposite direction: you start with specific routines and build them progressively into more complex structures, ending at the top-level routine. The *ad hoc* approach has no predetermined method. The top-down approach is generally considered to be the best and it is the only method that will be used here.

Top-down Programming

C as a structured language lends itself to a top-down approach. The top-down method can produce clean, readable code that can be easily maintained. A top-down approach also helps you clarify the overall structure and operation of the program before you code low-level functions. This can reduce time wasted by false starts.

Outlining Your Program

The top-down approach is similar to outlining, in which you start with the general idea and progressively define more of it at each lower level. A good way to start to code any program is to define exactly what the program is going to do at the top level. The definition of the Mailing List Program is

- Enter a new name
- Delete a name
- Print the list
- Search for a name
- Save the list to a disk file
- Load the list
- Quit the program.

These steps can form the basis of functions in the program.

After the overall function of the program has been defined, you can begin to sketch in the details of each functional area, beginning with the main loop. The main loop of this program is

```
main loop
{
    do {
        display menu
        get user selection
        process the selection
    } while selection does not equal quit
}
```

The use of this type of algorithmic notation can help you clarify the general structure of your program even before you sit down at the computer. C-type syntax has been used because it is familiar by now; however, any type of syntax is acceptable.

You should give a similar definition to each functional area. For example, the save-to-disk function can be defined as

```
save to disk {
    open disk file
    while data left to write {
        write data to disk
    }
    close disk file
}
```

Notice that the definition does not mention data structure or variables. This is intentional. At this point you are only interested in defining what your program will do, not how it will actually do it. This definition process will help you decide what the actual structure of the data should be.

Choosing a Data Structure

After you have determined the general outline to your program, the next step is to decide how the data used by your program will be stored. The selections of both the data structure and its implementation are critical because they help to determine the design limits of your program.

In earlier chapters, lists of information were represented as fixed-size arrays. For the Mailing List Program, a fixed-size array of structures could be used. However, a fixed-size array has two serious drawbacks in this case. First, the size of the array limits the length of the mailing list by placing an arbitrary limit on the program. Second, a fixed-size array will not take advantage of additional memory when added to your computer and, if memory is subtracted—for example, a memory card fails—the program may not work at all because the fixed-size array will not fit. Therefore, this Mailing List Program will use C's dynamic memory allocation functions **malloc( )** and **free( )** to allow the mailing list to be as large as free memory.

Although the storage method has been determined to be dynamic allocation, the exact form of the data still has not been decided. The program will use a structure, which will hold all of the address information and two pointers: one pointer to point to the next entry in the list and another to point to the previous entry in the list. Using two pointers per entry will make the mailing list a *doubly linked list*. This means that each entry will have pointers to the entry that precedes it and to the entry that follows it.

The structure for the address is

```
struct addr {
        char name[30];
        char street[40];
        char city[20];
        char state[3];
        char zip[10]; /* hold US and Canadian zips */
        struct addr *next;  /* pointer to next entry */
        struct addr *prior;  /* pointer to previous record */
} list_entry;
```

Each entry in the list will have the structure of **addr**. The two pointers in **addr** are of type **addr** because they will be pointing to structures of that type.

You must take care to choose descriptive names for the elements in the structure because it is the main data structure. Using descriptive names makes it easy to identify elements as you write your program.

One structure variable, **list—entry**, was also declared. This variable will help you later on in determining the size of the structure.

Figure 10-1 shows how a doubly linked list with elements of type **addr** will appear in memory. A doubly linked list has three tremendous advantages. First, to insert and delete entries into and from the list, all you have to do is switch the pointers. Second, the list can be read from front to back and from back to front. Third, a doubly linked list lends itself to rapid sorting because only the pointers have to be swapped, not the entire record.

A doubly linked list has two end points: its beginning and its end. The last element in the list must have its **next** pointer set to null, indicating that no other entries exist. The reverse case is also true: the first entry's **prior** pointer must be set to zero to indicate that no previous entries are present.

Both the general outline for the program and the structure of the data have now been defined. A good programmer should always think these two steps through carefully before beginning to code a program. This is the only way that well-written, reliable, easy-to-read programs can be developed consistently.

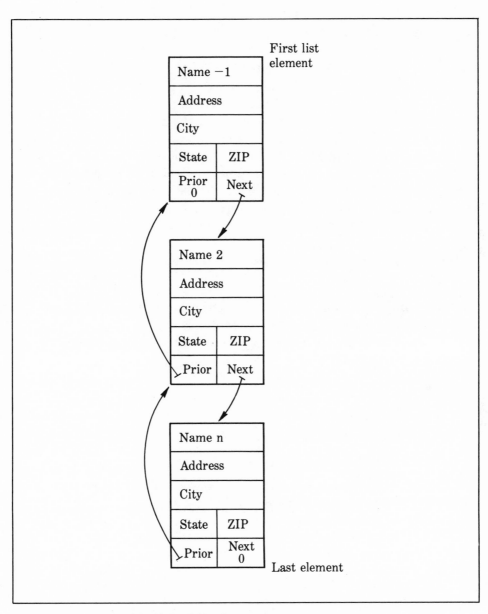

Figure 10-1. A doubly linked list in memory.

Defining the Global Variables
And the **main( )** Function

You are now ready to write the global variables and the **main( )** function. This Mailing List Program will only require two globals: the first to hold a pointer to the first entry in the list, and the second to hold a pointer to the last entry in the list. The start-of-list pointer tells the program where the first entry is. After that, the pointers in each entry will find the subsequent entries. The end-of-list pointer helps to speed up the entry routine. If the program keeps track of the end of list, adding a new address requires only updating a pointer on the old last entry to point to the new last entry. Otherwise, the program would have to scan the entire chain of entries to find the end.

The two pointer variables are

```
struct addr *start;  /* pointer to first entry in list */
struct addr *last;   /* pointer to last entry */
```

The **main( )** function is almost a direct translation from the outline. It is very easy for anyone reading the program to see exactly what the program does. The only initialization required is to set **start** to 0, which indicates an empty list.

```
main()
{
        int choice;

        start=0;  /* zero length list */
        do {
            choice=menu_select();
            switch(choice) {
                case 1: enter();  /* enter a new entry */
                        break;
                case 2: delete(); /* delete an existing entry */
                        break;
                case 3: list();   /* display the list */
                        break;
                case 4: search(); /* find an entry */
                        break;
                case 5: save();   /* save list to disk */
                        break;
                case 6: load();   /* read list from disk */
                        break;
                case 7: exit(0);
            }
        } while(1);
}
```

Even though descriptive names were chosen for the main functions **enter( )**, **delete( )**, **list( )**, **search( )**, **save( )**, and **load( )**, adding comments helps clarify what each case does. A person reading the program can easily find the correct function to examine in each program area.

The **menu—select( )** function is essentially the same as those used elsewhere in this book. You could write it like this:

```
menu_select()
{
        char s[80];
        int c;

        printf("1. Enter a name\n");
        printf("2. Delete a name\n");
        printf("3. List the file\n");
        printf("4. Search\n");
        printf("5. Save the file\n");
        printf("6. Load the file\n");
        printf("7. Quit\n");
        do {
                printf("\nEnter your choice: ");
                gets(s);
                c=atoi(s);
        } while(c<0 || c>7);
        return c;
}
```

It will prompt and loop until a valid selection is made.

When you write programs, remember that someone has to use them (this includes you). It is very important to trap invalid input. In this case, only a response that is between 1 and 7 is allowed. This helps prevent unpleasant surprises while using the program.

Defining enter

Because this Mailing List Program uses dynamic memory allocation to provide storage of the individual list entries, the **enter( )** routine must first allocate enough memory for the new entry. This program will use the standard function **malloc( )** to allocate memory. (Some compilers will call this **alloc( )**; be certain to check.) You could have counted the bytes to determine the size of structure **addr**, but C provides **sizeof**, which does this automatically. You need a pointer variable to hold the pointer returned by **malloc( )** and it must be declared as a pointer to **addr**. Here is **enter( )**:

```
enter()
{
        struct addr *info;
        char *malloc();

        do {
                info=malloc(sizeof(list_entry));
                if(info==0) {
                        printf("\nout of memory");
                        return;
                }

                inputs("enter name: ",info->name,30);
                if(!info->name[0]) break;  /* stop entering */
                inputs("enter street: ",info->street,40);
                inputs("enter city: ",info->city,20);
                inputs("enter state: ",info->state,3);
                inputs("enter zip: ",info->zip,10);

                if(start!=0) { /* if not first entry */
                        last->next=info;
                        info->prior=last;
                        last=info;
                        last->next=0;
                }
                else { /* is first entry */
                        start=info;
                        start->next=0;
                        last=start;

                        start->prior=0;
                }
        } while(1); /* entry loop */
}
```

Whenever **malloc( )** is used, you must verify that memory is available. The **malloc( )** will return either a valid memory address, which points to the start of the number of bytes requested, or 0, which indicates that the allocation failed because there was no free memory available. Failure to test for this condition can lead to catastrophic crashes. If you try to use the region of memory that starts at 0 on most systems, you will be writing over a portion of either the operating system, your program, or both. Be extremely careful about this. Also, notice that **malloc( )** is declared as returning a character pointer. Remember that C assumes that an integer is returned unless expressly declared otherwise.

Because it is so common to enter several addresses at one time, the **enter( )** function will loop until a blank line is entered at the name field.

Notice the use of the —> operator. Since all references to the mailing address information is through pointers, you have to use the arrow operator instead of the dot operator to access individual fields. This is further necessitated by the fact that the program uses dynamic storage for the list; dynamic storage cannot return a structure, only a memory address. By using a structure pointer, however, the C compiler can organize the block of memory received from **malloc( )** as if it were a structure variable.

Standard C does not have a prompting input function; however, this program needs to prompt the user for input and prevent boundary overflows in the string variables that make up each structure. A special function called **inputs( )** provides these services. It is a completely general function, except that the longest input line cannot exceed 255. The **inputs( )** function is written as

```
inputs(prompt,s,count) /* this function will input a string up to
                 the length in count.  This will prevent
                 the string from overrunning its space and
                 display a prompt message. */
char *prompt;
char *s;
int count;
{
        char p[255];

        do {
                printf(prompt);
                gets(p);
                if(strlen(p)>=count) printf("\ntoo long\n");
        } while(strlen(p)>=count);
        strcpy(s,p);
}
```

Notice that the input string is not entered directly into the argument, but is copied in only after the program determines that it will fit. This function is not completely foolproof because input longer than 255 will overwrite the local variable s. In the exercises, you will be asked to write a better version of **inputs( )** by rewriting **gets( )**, the standard C function.

Defining *delete( )*

The **delete( )** function is used to remove an entry from the mailing list. To remove an entry, you have to know the exact name. The **delete( )** will search the list until it either finds a match or reaches the end of the list. If it finds a match, that entry is deleted and the pointers of the preceding and following entries are updated so that they point "around" the deleted entry. The pointer to the memory region of the deleted entry is passed to **free( )**, the standard C function, which will return this unused memory back to the system for reuse later. The **delete( )** function is written as

```
delete()
{
        struct addr *info, *find();
        char s[255];

        inputs("enter name: ",s,30);
        info=find(s);
        if(info) {
                if(start==info) {
                        start=info->next;
                        start->prior=0;
                }
                else {
                        info->prior->next=info->next;
                        if(info!=last)
                            info->next->prior=info->prior;
                        else
                                last=info->prior;
                }
                free(info);  /* return memory to system */
        }
}
```

Notice that **inputs( )** was used to enter the name to be deleted. This is the advantage of a generalized function—it can be used over and over again. Notice also that **find( )** is declared as returning a pointer to a structure of type **addr.** Pay special attention to the pointer rearrangement code. Figure 10-2 shows how pointer changes take place after a deletion.

Consider this statement:

```
info->prior->next=info->next;
```

Since the arrow operator evaluates from left to right, the expression is the same as

```
(info->prior)->next=info->next;
```

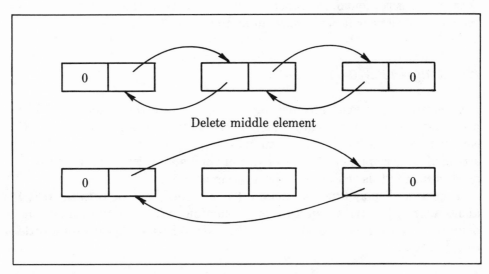

Figure 10-2.   Pointer changes after a deletion

This means that you will be assigning the value of the deleted entry's **next** pointer to the preceding entry's **next** pointer.

The **find( )** function is a linear search of the list. It starts at the beginning of the list and stops either at the end or at the entry that matches the entered name. The end of the list is recognized when the **next** pointer is 0. The **find( )** function is written as

```
struct addr *
find(name)
char *name;
{
        struct addr *info;

        info=start;
        while(info) {
                if(!strcmp(name,info->name)) return info;
                info=info->next;   /* get next entry */
        }
        printf("name not found\n");
        return 0;   /* not found */
}
```

If the name is not found, the function returns a 0 because a validly allocated region of memory will never have an address of 0.

Printing the Mailing List

Most mailing lists generate mailing labels. Because the exact method of accessing the printer can vary widely based on the operating system and C compiler you are using, this program will simply print the mailing list to the screen of your computer. As one of this chapter's exercises, you are encouraged to modify this routine to print to your printer.

A general display function, **display( )**, is needed because both the **list( )** and **search( )** functions require it to display information on the screen. The **display( )** function is used to shorten the code in **list( )** and make it a little easier to read:

```
list()
{
        register int t;
        struct addr *info;

        info=start;
        while(info) {
                display(info);
                info=info->next;  /* get next entry */
        }
        printf("\n\n");
}

display(info)
struct addr *info;
{
                printf("%s\n",info->name);
                printf("%s\n",info->street);
                printf("%s\n",info->city);
                printf("%s\n",info->state);
                printf("%s\n",info->zip);
                printf("\n\n");
}
```

Finding a Name in the Mailing List

A mailing list is often used to look up a person's address. The **search( )** function can accomplish this. To use **search( )**, you enter the name of the person that you want to find. In **search( )**, **inputs( )** is used to input the name:

```
search()
{
        char name[30];
        struct addr *info,*find();

        inputs("enter name to find: ",name,30);
        if(!(info=find(name))) printf("not found\n");
        else display(info);
}
```

Saving and Loading the List

To save the mailing list to disk, the function **save( )** is needed. In this simple version of **save( )**, the name **mlist** is permanently coded as the filename.

```
save()
{
        register int t,size;
        struct addr *info;
        char *p;
        FILE *fp;

        if((fp=fopen("mlist","w"))==0) {
                printf("cannot open file\n");
                exit(0);
        }

        printf("\nsaving file\n");
        size=sizeof(list_entry);
        info=start;
        while(info) {
                p=info;  /* convert to char pointer */
                for(t=0;t<size;++t)
                        putc(*p++,fp);  /* save byte at a time */
                info=info->next;  /* get next address */
        }
        putc(EOF,fp);  /* send an explicit EOF */
        fclose(fp);
}
```

The function begins at the top of the list and goes to the end, writing out all of the bytes in each structure using **putc( )**, the standard library function. The character pointer **p** is assigned the location of the start of each structure, and **sizeof(list—entry)** controls the number of bytes to write. Although most of the information in the file is printable, the pointers will not be, so you should not try to print this file to your screen or printer.

The **load( )** function is a bit more complicated. It must actually build the list and set all pointers as it reads in the data.

```
load()
{
        register int t,size;
        struct addr *info, *temp;
        char *p, *malloc();
        FILE *fp;

        if((fp=fopen("mlist","r"))==0) {
                printf("cannot open file\n");
                exit(0);
        }

        printf("\nloading file\n");
        size=sizeof(list_entry);
        start=malloc(size);
        if(!start) {
                printf("out of memory\n");
                return;
        }
        info=start;
        p=info;  /* convert to char pointer */

        while((*p++=getc(fp))!=EOF) {
                for(t=0;t<size-1;++t)
                        *p++=getc(fp);   /* load byte at a time */
                info->next=malloc(size); /* get memory for next */
                if(!info->next) {

                        printf("out of memory\n");
                        return;
                }
                info->prior=temp;
                temp=info;
                info=info->next;
                p=info;
        }
        free(temp->next);   /* release unused memory */
        temp->next=0;  /* last entry */
        last=temp;
        start->prior=0;
        fclose(fp);
}
```

Limitations

Several limitations have been designed into this Mailing List Program. Most keep the example simple, while some were specific design decisions. A good programmer must be aware of both the limitations as well as the capabilities of the program.

One obvious limitation of the program is in the data structure itself. There is only room for one name and one street. This is fine for most home addresses, but often businesses have two names and two street lines. A second name line can also allow a "to the attention of" line. Because everything in the program is dynamic and because the program used **sizeof** when the actual size of the structure was needed, all you have to do to add more room is to add fields to the data structure and to the functions **enter( )** and **display( )**.

A frequently asked question about this type of program is, How many entries can it store? Because the program uses dynamic storage, there is no absolute answer. The number of entries is limited by the amount of free memory in the system. You could get a rough estimate of the number of entries by dividing the size of **addr** into the free memory. But remember that other functions in the program—including the disk file functions—are also making demands on memory.

Currently the program has no way of sorting the mailing list. In this sense, the design of the program may not meet the needs of most users. However, this limitation may not matter to someone who does not want a sorted list. It is important to remember for whom you are writing a program. Even if you will be the final user, your program must satisfy your needs as well.

Problems With the Mailing List Program

If you enter and compile all of the functions listed in this chapter, you will have a Mailing List Program that operates as described. It *will* work. It lacks resiliency to certain types of hardware failures as it stands and contains at least one bug.

The resiliency problem has to do with the way in which the pointers are rearranged in **delete( )**. All programmers must recognize the fact that hardware fails from time to time. If a memory error occurs in the middle of the deletion process, it is possible to lose all entries after the deleted entry. The deleted point is disconnected from the chain. However, memory error causes the **next** pointer to drop a bit, making it point to some unknown region of memory. This invalid pointer is now put into the **next** pointer of the preceding entry. This causes the chain to be broken. Although it is impossible to eliminate this type of problem completely, adding a redundancy check to the code would trap most of these errors and inform the user of a problem.

It is the responsibility of the programmer to make the hardware perform as well as possible, even if that means anticipating potential hardware problems.

The bug in the program was left in intentionally. Examine the **load( )** routine closely. What will happen on repeated calls to this function? Try to find the bug before you read further.

The answer is that eventually memory will be completely used up because it is not freed prior to the load. Each load continues to allocate new memory; if you loaded the same list twice, you would be allocating a separate region of memory for each load. The solution is to write a function called **fre—list( )** that will release the memory for any list currently in use. This is the subject of an exercise.

The Complete Mailing List Program

The entire Mailing List Program is listed in Figure 10-3.

```
struct addr {
        char name[30];
        char street[40];
        char city[20];
        char state[3];
        char zip[10]; /* hold US and Canadian zips */
        struct addr *next;  /* pointer to next entry */
        struct addr *prior;  /* pointer to previous record */
} list_entry;

struct addr *start;  /* pointer to first entry in list */
struct addr *last;  /* pointer to last entry */

main()
{
        int choice;

        start=0;  /* zero length list */
        do {
```

Figure 10-3. The complete Mailing List Program

```
                    choice=menu_select();
                    switch(choice) {
                        case 1: enter();  /* enter a new entry */
                               break;
                        case 2: delete(); /* delete an existing entry */
                               break;
                        case 3: list();   /* display the list */
                               break;
                        case 4: search(); /* find an entry */
                               break;
                        case 5: save();   /* save list to disk */
                               break;
                        case 6: load();   /* read list from disk */
                               break;
                        case 7: exit(0);
                    }
                } while(1);
        }


        menu_select()
        {
                char s[80];
                int c;

                printf("1. Enter a name\n");
                printf("2. Delete a name\n");
                printf("3. List the file\n");
                printf("4. Search\n");
                printf("5. Save the file\n");
                printf("6. Load the file\n");
                printf("7. Quit\n");
                do {
                        printf("\nEnter your choice: "):
                        gets(s);
                        c=atoi(s);
                } while(c<0 || c>7);
                return c;
        }

        enter()
        {
                struct addr *info;
                char *malloc();
                do {
                        info=malloc(sizeof(list_entry));
                        if(info==0) {
                                printf("\nout of memory");
                                return;
                        }

                        inputs("enter name: ",info->name,30);
                        if(!info->name[0]) break;  /* stop entering */
                        inputs("enter street: ",info->street,40);
                        inputs("enter city: ",info->city,20);
                        inputs("enter state: ",info->state,3);
                        inputs("enter zip: ",info->zip,10);

                        if(start!=0) {  /* if not first entry */
```

Figure 10-3. The complete Mailing List Program (*continued*)

```
                          last->next=info;
                          info->prior=last;
                          last=info;
                          last->next=0;
                  }
                  else {  /* is first entry */
                          start=info;
                          start->next=0; .
                          last=start;

                          start->prior=0;
                  }
          } while(1); /* entry loop */
}

inputs(prompt,s,count) /* this function will input a string up to
                   the length in count.  This will prevent
                   the string from overrunning its space and
                   display a prompt message. */
char *prompt;
char *s;
int count;
{
        char p[255];
        do {
                printf(prompt);
                gets(p);
                if(strlen(p)>=count) printf("\ntoo long\n");
        } while(strlen(p)>=count);
        strcpy(s,p);

}

delete()
{
        struct addr *info, *find();
        char s[255];

        inputs("enter name: ",s,30);
        info=find(s);
        if(info) {
                if(start==info) {
                        start=info->next;
                        start->prior=0;
                }
                else {
                        info->prior->next=info->next;
                        if(info!=last)
                            info->next->prior=info->prior;
                        else
                                last=info->prior;
                }
                free(info);  /* return memory to system */
        }
}

struct addr *find(name)
char *name;
{
        struct addr *info;
```

Figure 10-3. The complete Mailing List Program (*continued*)

```
            info=start;
            while(info) {
                    if(!strcmp(name,info->name)) return info;
                    info=info->next;   /* get next entry */
            }
            printf("name not found\n");
            return 0;  /* not found */
}

list()
{
            register int t;
            struct addr *info;

            info=start;
            while(info) {
                    display(info);
                    info=info->next;   /* get next entry */
            }
            printf("\n\n");
}

display(info)
struct addr *info;
{
                    printf("%s\n",info->name);
                    printf("%s\n",info->street);
                    printf("%s\n",info->city);
                    printf("%s\n",info->state);
                    printf("%s\n",info->zip);
                    printf("\n\n");
}

search()
{
            char name[30];
            struct addr *info,*find();

            inputs("enter name to find: ",name,30);
            if(!(info=find(name))) printf("not found\n");
            else display(info);
}

save()
{
            register int t,size;
            struct addr *info;
            char *p;
            FILE *fp;

            if((fp=fopen("mlist","w"))==0) {
                    printf("cannot open file\n");
                    exit(0);
            }

            printf("\nsaving file\n");
            size=sizeof(list_entry);
            info=start;
```

Figure 10-3. The complete Mailing List Program (*continued*)

```
            while(info) {
                    p=info;  /* convert to char pointer */
                    for(t=0;t<size;++t)
                                putc(*p++,fp);  /* save byte at a time */
                    info=info->next;  /* get next address */
            }
            putc(EOF,fp);  /* send an explicit EOF */
            fclose(fp);
    }

    load()
    {
            register int t,size;
            struct addr *info, *temp;
            char *p, *malloc();
            FILE *fp;

            if((fp=fopen("mlist","r"))==0) {
                    printf("cannot open file\n");
                    exit(0);
            }

            printf("\nloading file\n");
            size=sizeof(list_entry);
            start=malloc(size);
            if(!start) {
                    printf("out of memory\n");
                    return;
            }
            info=start;
            p=info;  /* convert to char pointer */

            while((*p++=getc(fp))!=EOF) {
                    for(t=0;t<size-1;++t)
                                *p++=getc(fp);  /* load byte at a time */
                    info->next=malloc(size); /* get memory for next */
                    if(!info->next) {

                            printf("out of memory\n");
                            return;
                    }
                    info->prior=temp;
                    temp=info;
                    info=info->next;
                    p=info;
            }
            free(temp->next);  /* release unused memory */
            temp->next=0;  /* last entry */
            last=temp;
            start->prior=0;
            fclose(fp);
    }
```

Figure 10-3.   The complete Mailing List Program (*continued*)

E X E R C I S E S

1. Compile and run the Mailing List Program described in this chapter.

2. Rewrite the structure **addr** so that it accommodates two name fields.

3. Rewrite **list( )** for your computer so that it will print the addresses to your printer.

4. Write the function **fre_list( )**, which will release all currently allocated memory back to the system.

A N S W E R S

```
2. struct addr {
          char name[30];
          char name2[30];
          char street[40];
          char city[20];
          char state[3];
          char zip[10]; /* hold US and Canadian zips */
          struct addr *next;   /* pointer to next entry */
          struct addr *prior;  /* pointer to previous record */
   } list_entry;


4. fre_list()
   {
          struct addr *info, *temp;
          info=start;
          while(info) {
                  temp=info->next;
                  free(info);
                  info=temp;
          }
   }
```

Common Programming Errors

CHAPTER 11

Although it is rare to find a chapter devoted to common programming errors in a book teaching a programming language, such a chapter is necessary in this book because C has certain qualities that can create bugs not usually found in other programming languages.

C is very robust: it has very little run-time error checking or reporting built directly into the language. Unlike BASIC, which, when a disk request fails, will issue a message saying **cannot open file**, C will simply do nothing unless you have expressly checked for that condition in your program.

Types of Errors

Generally, when a program does not run correctly, there are a few possible reasons, which fall into three categories.

- Hardware failures
- User-input data errors
- Software errors.

As the programmer, you must determine where the error is and then fix it. Of these three possible error categories, input errors and software errors are directly under your control; if the hardware fails, you are only responsible for demonstrating the failure conclusively so that it can be fixed. Your programs should trap user-input errors before they cause problems. Finally, it is directly your responsibility to produce bug-free code, without any errors in syntax, implementation, or design.

You should have the expertise to correct most syntax errors reported by your compiler. But having a syntactically correct program is only the first step. Your program must do what you think it is going to do. The rest of this chapter discusses the most common ways errors can creep into your code plus a few unusual syntax errors.

Order of Process Errors

The increment and decrement operators are used in most programs written in C. You should remember, however, that the order in which the operation takes place is affected by whether these operators precede or follow the variable. For example, these two statements

```
y=10;
x=y++;
```

and

```
y=10;
x=++y;
```

are not the same. The first one assigns the value of 10 to **x** and then increments **y**. The second increments **y** to 11 and then assigns the value 11 to **x**. Therefore, in the first case, **x** contains 10; in the second, **x** contains 11.

The increment and decrement operations will occur before other operations if they precede the operand; otherwise, they will occur afterwards.

This type of mix-up can be very hard to find. There may be clues, such as loops that don't run correctly or routines that are off by 1. Make sure that you understand the increment and decrement operators.

Pointer Problems

A common error in C programs is the misuse of pointers. Pointer problems fall into two categories: the first is a misunderstanding of indirection and the pointer operators; the second is the accidental use of invalid pointers. The solution to the first problem is to review the C language, making sure you understand how you have set up the program; the solution to the second problem is to always verify the validity of a pointer before it is used.

Figure 11-1 shows a program with typical pointer errors that beginning C programmers make. This program will most likely crash, probably also taking the operating system with it. The reason it does not work is that the address returned by **malloc( )** was assigned *not to* **p**, but rather to the memory location that **p** points to, which is completely unknown in this case. This is certainly not what is wanted. To correct this program, you must substitute

```
p=malloc(100); /* this is correct */
```

for the line that is wrong.

The program has a second, more insidious error. There is no run-time check on the address returned by **malloc( )**. Remember that if memory is exhausted, **malloc( )** will return 0, which is never a valid pointer in C. The malfunction caused by this type of bug is difficult to find because it will only

```
main()   /* this program is WRONG */
{
        char *p;
        char *alloc();
        *p=malloc(100); /* this line is wrong */
        gets(p);
        printf(p);
}
```

Figure 11-1. A program showing typical pointer errors

```
main()   /* this program is now correct */
{
        char *p;
        char *alloc();
        p=malloc(100);  /* this is correct */
        if(p==0)  {
                printf("out of  memory\n");
                exit(0);
        }
        gets(p);
        printf(p);
}
```

Figure 11-2. Corrected version of the program in Figure 11-1.

occur rarely, when an allocation request fails. The best way to handle this is to prevent it. Figure 11-2 gives a corrected version of the program, which includes a check for pointer validity.

The terrible thing about "wild" pointers is that they are so hard to track down. If you are making assignments to a pointer variable that does not contain a valid pointer address, your program may appear to function correctly some of the time and crash at other times. The smaller your program, the more likely it will run correctly, even with a stray pointer, because very little memory is in use. As your program grows, failures will become more common, but you may think that the error lies in the current additions or changes to your program, not in the pointers. Hence, you will tend to look in the wrong spot for the bug.

One sign of a pointer problem is that errors tend to be erratic. Your program will work correctly one time and incorrectly another time. Sometimes other variables will contain garbage for no explainable reason. If these problems begin to occur, check your pointers.As a matter of procedure, be certain to check all pointers when bugs begin to occur.

Remember, however, that while pointers can be troublesome, they are also one of the most powerful and useful aspects of the C language and worth whatever trouble they may cause. Make an effort to learn to use them correctly.

One final point about pointers: you must initialize them before they are used. This may seem simple enough to remember, but many excellent C programmers still forget from time to time. For example, this fragment

```
int *x;
*x=100;
```

will cause a disaster because you don't know where **x** is pointing to. Assigning a value to that unknown location is probably destroying something of value—like other code or data for your program.

Redefining Functions

You can, but should not, call your functions by the same names as those in the C standard library. Most compilers will use your function over the one in the library. This can cause problems directly and indirectly.

For example, these program fragments show a direct problem caused by redefining a library function:

```
main( )
{
    FILE *fp;
    char big[1000];
    init_array(big);
    if((fp=open("name","r"))==-1) {
        printf("cannot open file \n");
        exit(0);
    }
    .
    .
    .
}
init_array(s)
char *s;
{
    register int t;
    for(t=0;t<1000; t++,p++) {
        *p=t;
        if(t%100) open(p);
    }
}
open(p)
char *p;
{
    *p='O';
}
```

The standard function **open( )** has been redefined in the program to assign the character **O** to certain elements of an array. It has nothing to do with the **open( )** used to open a disk file which is called in **main( )**. Using **open( )** in this way will cause the program to either crash or do bizarre things.

A worse problem occurs when a standard library function is redefined, but the standard function is used indirectly by another standard function. For example,

```
char text[1000];
main( )
{
    int x;
    scanf("%d",&x);
    .

    .

    .
}
getc(p) /* return char from array */
{
    return text[p];
}
    .

    .

    .
```

This program will not work with most compilers because **scanf( )**, a standard C function, will probably call **getc( )**, another standard C function, which has been redefined in the program. This can be a very frustrating problem because there won't be a clue that you have created a side effect. It will simply seem that **scanf( )** is not working correctly.

The only way to avoid these problems is by never giving a function that you write the same name as one in the standard library. If you are unsure, append your initials to the beginning of the name, such as **hs_getc( )** instead of **getc( )**.

Bizarre Syntax Errors

Once in a while, the C compiler may report a syntax error that you may not recognize as being an error at all, because the C compiler itself may have a bug that causes it to report false errors. The only solution is to redesign your code. Other unusual errors simply require some backtracking on your part.

One particularly unsettling error will occur when you try to compile code containing this fragment:

```
main( )
{
    char *p, *myfunc( );  /* myfunc( ) returns
                                       char pointer */
    .
    .
    .
}
myfunc( )
{
    .
    .
    .
}
```

Most compilers will issue an error message such as **function redefined** and point to **myfunc( )**. How can this be? The code does not have two **myfunc( )**s. The answer is that you declared **myfunc( )** to be returning a character pointer inside **main( )**. This caused a symbol table entry to be made with that information: when the compiler encountered **myfunc( )** later in the program, there was no indication that it was to return anything other than an integer, the default type. Hence, you were "redefining" the function. The correction would be

```
main( )
{
    char *p, *myfunc( ); /* myfunc( ) returns
                                      char pointer */
    .
    .
    .
}
char *myfunc( )
{
    .
    .
    .
}
```

Figure 11-3 lists a program with another syntax error that is difficult to understand. The error in this program is the semicolon after the declaration

```
main() /* this program has a syntax error in it */
{
        func1();
}
func1();
{
        printf("this is func1 \n");
}
```

Figure 11-3.   A program with an unusual syntax error

of **func1( )**. The compiler will see this as a statement outside of any function, which is an error. However, the way that various compilers report this error will differ. Many compilers will issue an error message like **bad declaration syntax** while pointing at the first open brace after **func1( )**. Because you are used to seeing semicolons after statements, it can be very hard to see where this error is coming from.

Indexing Errors

As you should know by now, all C indexes start at 0. A common error involves the use of a **for** loop to access the elements of an array.

Figure 11-4 gives a program that is supposed to initialize an array of 100 integers. The **for** loop in this program is wrong in two ways: first, it will not

```
main()   /* this program will not work */
{
        int x, num[100];
        for (x=1; x<=100; ++x) num[x]=x;
}
```

Figure 11-4.   A program that incorrectly uses a **for** loop to initialize an array

```
main()   /* this is right */
{
        int x, num[100];
        for (x=0; x<100; ++x) num[x]=x;
}
```

Figure 11-5. Corrected version of the program in Figure 11-4

initialize **num[0]**, the first element of array **num**; and second, the loop runs to 100, one past the last element in the array, **num[99]**. The correct way to write this program is shown in Figure 11-5. Remember, an array of 100 has elements 0 through 99.

Boundary Errors

C and many standard library functions have very little or no run-time bounds checking. For example, it is possible to overwrite arrays, disk files, and, through pointer assignments, any variable. These errors usually do not occur, but when they do, linking the symptom with the cause can be very difficult.

For example, the program in Figure 11-6 is supposed to read a string from the keyboard and display it on the screen. Here there are no direct coding errors. Indirectly, however, calling **get_string( )** with **s** will cause a bug. The variable **s** is declared to be 10 characters long, but **get_string( )** will read 20 characters. This will cause **s** to be overwritten. The real problem is that while **s** may display all 20 characters correctly, **var1** or **var2** will not contain the correct value.

The reason for this problem lies in the way the compiler uses memory. All C compilers must allocate a region of memory for local variables. This is usually the stack region. The variables **var1**, **s**, and **var2** will be located in memory as shown in Figure 11-7. Your C compiler may exchange the order of **var1** and **var2**, but they will still bracket **s**. When **s** is overwritten, the additional information is placed into the area that is supposed to be reserved for **var2**, destroying any previous contents. Therefore, instead of printing the number 10 for both integer variables, the one destroyed by the overrun of **s**

```
            main()
            {
                int var1;
                char s[10];
                int var2;
                var1=10;   var2=10;
                get_string(s);
                printf("%s %d %s",s,var1,var2);
            }
            get_string(string)
            char *string;
            {
                register int t;
                printf("enter twenty characters\n");
                for(t=0;t<20;++t) {
                        *s++=getchar();
                }
            }
```

Figure 11-6.   A program that will overwrite a variable

will display something else. Seeing this may cause you to look for the problem in the wrong place.

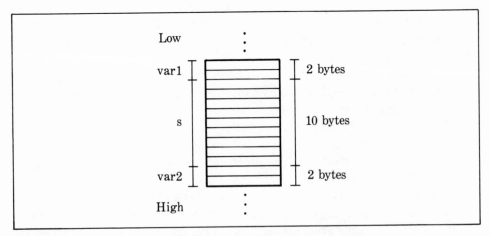

Figure 11-7.   Local variables **var1**, s, and **var2** in a stack

```
      main()   /* this is wrong */
      {
            float x,y;
            scanf("%f%f",&x,&y);
            printf("%f",mul(x,y));
      }
      float mul(a,b)
      float a,b;
      {
            return a*b;
      }
```

Figure 11-8. A program that is missing a function declaration

Function Declaration Omissions

Any time a function returns a value type other than integer, the function must be declared inside each function that uses it. An example of what happens when a function declaration is missing is the program in Figure 11-8, which multiplies two floating point numbers together.

In this program, **main( )** will expect an integer value back from **mul( )**, but **mul( )** will return a floating point number. You will get meaningless answers because **main( )** will only copy two bytes out of the eight needed for a **float**.

The way to correct this program is to declare **mul( )** in **main( )**, as shown in Figure 11-9. The **mul( )** function has been added to the **float** declaration list, which tells **main( )** to expect a floating point value to be returned from **mul( )**.

Calling Argument Errors

You must match every type of argument a function expects with the type you give it. An important example is **scanf( )**. Remember that **scanf( )** expects to receive the *address* of its arguments, not the value. This means that you must

```
        main()   /* this is correct */
        {
             float x,y,mul();
             scanf("%f%f",&x,&y);
             printf"%f",mul(x,y));
        }
        float mul(a,b)
        float a,b;
        {
             return a*b;
        }
```

Figure 11-9.   Corrected version of the program in Figure 11-8.

call **scanf( )** with arguments using the **&** operator. For example,

```
int x;
char string[10];
scanf("%d%s",x,string);
```

is wrong, while

```
scanf("%d%s",&x,string);
```

is correct. Remember, though, that strings already pass their addresses to functions, so you should not use the **&** operator on them.

Another common error is to forget that, unless explicitly done otherwise, C functions cannot modify their arguments. If it is necessary to modify an argument to a function, you must pass the address of the argument to the function and use pointer references to access it.

If a function's formal parameters are of type **float**, you must pass floating point variables to the function. For example, in the program in Figure 11-10, you cannot use a floating-point function such as **div( )** to return an integer value. Furthermore, **div( )** will not operate correctly because it is expecting floating point numbers, not integers.

```
main() /* this program is wrong */
{
        int x,y;
        scanf("%d%d",x,y,);
        printf("%d",div(x,y));
}
float div(a,b)
float a,b;
{
        return a/b;
}
```

Figure 11-10. A program that shows a calling argument error

Incremental Testing

Everyone has a different approach to programming and debugging. However, certain techniques have over time proven to be better than others. In the case of debugging, *incremental testing* is considered to be the most cost-effective method, even though it can appear to slow the development process at first.

Incremental testing is simply the process of always having working code. As soon as it is possible to run a piece of your program, you should do so to test that section completely. As you add to the program, continue to test the new sections, scrutinizing the way they connect to the earlier tested sections. In this way, you will be concentrating any possible bugs into a small area of code.

Incremental testing theory is generally based on probability and areas. As you know, area is a squared dimension. Each time that you add length, you double area. Therefore, as your program grows, there is an N-squared area you must search for bugs. As a programmer, you want the smallest possible area to work with while debugging. Through incremental testing, you are able to subtract the area already tested from the total area, thereby reducing the region where a bug may be found.

One final thought: perfection is attainable only as an accident; therefore, good programmers are also good debuggers.

E X E R C I S E S

1. What is wrong with the following code fragment?

```
/* assign numbers 0 through 9 to num */
int t, num[10];
t=0;
do
        num[t]=++t;
}while(t<10);
```

2. What is wrong with this program?

```
main()
{
        char *c;
        int t;
        c=&t;
        *c=10;
}
```

3. Why won't this program work? Show how to fix it.

```
main()   /* swap two integers */
{
        int a,b;
        a=10;   b=20;
        swap(a,b);
}
swap(x,y)
```

```
int x,y;
{
        int temp;
        temp=x;
        x=y;
        y=temp;
}
```

4. Will this program ever terminate?

```
main()
{
        int t;
        for(t=0; t!=10;++t) {
                printf("%d",t);
                if(t==10) t=0;
        }
}
```

5. What is wrong in this code fragment?

```
int x;
scanf("%f",x);
```

A N S W E R S

1. Because **t** is incremented prior to being assigned, the numbers 1 through 10 will be placed into array **num**. The assignment line should be

```
num[t]=t++;
```

2. The program is attempting to assign, using indirection, an integer value by using a character pointer. This may be desired under certain very special circumstances, but as this program stands, it is considered an error.

3. C uses call by value, which implies that the arguments to functions cannot be changed by those functions. To correct this program, both the call to **mul( )** and **mul( )** itself must be changed to accept pointers. When corrected, the program is

```
main()   /* swap two integers */
{
        int a,b;
        a=10;   b=20;
        swap(&a,&b);
}
swap(x,y)
int x,y;
{
        int temp;
        temp=*x;
        x=*y;
        y=temp;
}
```

4. No.

5. Two things are wrong: first, **x** is an integer and **scanf( )** is being told to read a floating point number; second, **scanf( )** needs to be called with the *address* of the variable, not its value.

C Summary

A P P E N D I X   A

C has 28 keywords. These words, combined with the formal C syntax, form the C programming language. Here is a list of all the C keywords:

auto	double	if	static
break	else	int	struct
case	entry	long	switch
char	extern	register	typedef
continue	float	return	union
default	for	sizeof	unsigned
do	goto	short	while

Statement Summary

This section summarizes many common C statements and provides examples of how they can be used.

break

A **break** is used to exit from a **do, for,** or **while** loop, bypassing the normal loop condition. It is also used to exit from a **switch** statement.

This is an example of **break** in a loop:

```
while(x<100) {
    x=get_new_x();
    if(keystroke()) break;  /* key hit on keyboard */
    process(x);
}
```

If a key is typed, the loop will terminate, no matter what the value of **x** is.

In a **switch** statement, **break** effectively keeps program execution from "falling through" to the next **case**. (Refer to the **switch** statement for details.)

continue

A **continue** is used to bypass portions of code in a loop and force the conditional test to be performed. For example, this **while** loop will read characters from the keyboard until an **s** is typed:

```
while(ch=getchar) {
    if(ch!='s') continue: /* read another char */
    process(ch);
}
```

The call to **process( )** will not occur until **ch** contains the character **s**.

do

The **do** loop is one of three loop constructs available in C. The general form of the **do** loop is

```
do {
    statement block
} while(condition);
```

If only one statement is repeated, the braces are not necessary, but they do add clarity to the statement.

The **do** loop is the only loop in C that will always have at least one iteration because the condition is tested at the bottom of the loop.

A common use of the **do** loop is reading disk files. This code will read a file until an **EOF** is encountered:

```
do {
    ch=getc(fp);
    store(ch);
} while(ch!=EOF);
```

for

The **for** loop allows automatic initialization and incrementation of a counter variable. The general form is

```
for(initialization; condition; increment) {
    statement block
}
```

If the statement block is only a single statement, the braces are not necessary.

Although the **for** allows a number of variations, the initialization is generally used to set a counter variable to its starting value. The condition is usually a relational statement that checks the counter variable against a termination value, and the increment increments (or decrements) the counter value.

This code will print the message **hello** ten times.

```
for(t=0;t<10;++t) printf("hello\n");
```

The next code will wait for a keystroke after printing **hello**.

```
for(t=0;t<10;t++) {
    printf("hello\n");
    getchar();
}
```

goto

The **goto** causes program execution to "jump" to the label specified in the **goto** statement. The general form of the **goto** is

goto label;
.
.
.
label:

All labels must end in a colon and must not conflict with keywords or function names.

For example, this code will print the message **right**, but not the message **wrong**.

```
goto lab1;
      printf("wrong");
lab1:
      printf("right");
```

if and else

The general form of the **if** statement is

```
if(condition) {
      statement block 1
}
else {
      statement block 2
}
```

If single statements are used, the braces are not needed. The **else** is optional.

The condition may be any expression. If that expression evaluates to any value other than 0, statement block 1 will be executed; otherwise, if it exists, statement block 2 will be executed.

This fragment can be used for keyboard input and to look for a **q**, which signifies "quit":

```
ch=getchar();
if(ch=='q') {
    printf("program terminated");
    exit(0);
}
else proceed();
```

return

The **return** statement forces a return from a function and can be used to transfer a value back to the calling routine. For example, the following function returns the product of its two integer arguments:

```
mul(a,b)
int a,b;
{
    return(a*b);
}
```

Keep in mind that as soon as a **return** is encountered, the function will return, skipping any other code in the function.

switch

The **switch** statement is C's multidirection branch statement: it is used to route execution one of several different ways. The general form of the statement is

```
switch(variable) {
    case (constant1): statement set 1;
                      break;
    case (constant2): statement set 1;
                      break;
        .
        .
        .
    case (constant n): statement set n;
                       break;
    default: default statements;
}
```

Each statement set may be from one to several statements long. The **default** portion is optional.

The **switch** works by checking the variable against all the constants. As soon as a match is found, that set of statements is executed. You can think of the **cases** as labels. If the **break** statement is omitted, execution will continue until a **break** statement is found or until the **switch** ends.

The following example can be used to process a menu selection:

```
ch=getchar();
switch (ch) {
    case 'e': enter();
              break;
    case 'l': list();
              break;
    case 's': sort();
              break;
    case 'q': exit(0);
    default: printf("unknown command\n");
              printf("try again\n");
```

while

The **while** loop has the general form

```
while(condition) {
    statement block
}
```

If a single statement is the object of the **while**, the braces may be omitted.

The **while** tests its condition at the top of the loop. Therefore, if the condition is false to begin with, the loop may not execute at all. The condition may be any expression.

In this example of a **while**, 100 characters will be read from a disk file and stored into a character array:

```
t=0;
while (t<100) {
    s[t]=getc(fp);
    t++;
}
```

Data Types

C has the following built-in data types:

C keyword	type
character	char
integer	int
long integer	long int
short integer	short int
unsigned integer	unsigned int
floating point	float
double floating point	double

In addition to the built-in types, you can create combinations of them using **struct** and **union**. You can also create new names for variable types using **typedef**.

The general form of a **struct** declaration is

```
struct struct_name {
    element 1;
    element 2;
        .
        .
        .
} struct_variable;
```

The general form for a **union** is

```
union union_name {
    element 1;
    element 2;
        .
        .
        .
} union_variable;
```

You may declare variables to be **static**, which makes them stay in existence throughout the entire program execution.

The **register** modifier can be used on integers and characters. It causes the specified variables to be stored in a register of the CPU instead of in a memory location. This makes access to those variables much faster.

If **extern** is placed before a variable name, the compiler will know that that variable has to be declared elsewhere. The most common use of this is when you have two or more files sharing the same global variables.

Common C
Library Functions

A P P E N D I X   B

The functions described in this appendix will be found in the standard libraries of most C compilers. The descriptions here will serve as a general guide to their use; however, consult your user manual for exact details.

atoi(p)
char *p;

The **atoi( )** converts a string of digits into their integer value. The **atoi( )** function has a single character pointer argument that points to the string of digits. The integer value of that argument is returned. If the string passed to **atoi( )** does not contain a valid integer number, a 0 will be returned. Leading spaces and tabs are generally ignored and a minus sign may be used.

The following program will input a number from the keyboard and convert it to an integer:

```
main()
{
        register int n;
        char s[80];
        printf("enter a number: ");
        gets(s);
        n=atoi(s);
}
```

close(fd)
int fd;

The **close( )** is used to close a disk file that had been opened when using **open( )** or **creat( )**. It is part of the unbuffered I/O file system. A **close( )** will return 0 if the operation is successful.

The file descriptor **fd** is an integer returned by the call to **open( )** or **creat( )**.

The following program opens a file called **test** for unbuffered I/O and then closes it:

```
main()
{
        int fd;
        char buf[128];
        if((fd=open("test",0))==-1) {
                printf("cannot open file.\n");
                exit(1);
        }
        read(fd,buf,128);   /* read one buffer */
        close(fd);
}
```

creat(name,mode)
char *name;
int mode;

A **creat( )** is used to create a new file and open it for write operations. The **creat( )** function is part of the unbuffered I/O file system.

The character string **name** must be a pointer to a valid file name; **mode** specifies the protection mode and is optional on most microcomputer C implementations.

If **creat( )** is successful in opening a new file, it returns a file descriptor; otherwise, it will return a −1, which indicates a failure.

If a file of the same name already exists, it will be erased, so exercise care when using **creat( )**.

The following function will create and open a user-defined file for write operations and return the file descriptor.

```
cr_file()
{
        char name[80];
        int fd;
        printf("enter filename: ");
        gets(name);
        if((fd=creat(name,0))==-1) {
                printf("cannot open file\n");
                return -1;
        }
        return fd;
}
```

fclose(fp)
FILE *fp;

The **fclose( )** is part of the buffered I/O file system. It is used to write any data remaining in the buffer to the file and close the file. The file must have previously been opened using **fopen( )**, the buffered I/O open function. The file pointer is **fp**, previously returned by the call to **fopen( )**.

If **fclose( )** is successful, it returns 0; otherwise, it returns −1.

For example, this program opens a file for buffered write operations and closes it; only one character is written to the file.

```
main()
{
        FILE fp;
        if((fp=fopen("test","w"))==0) {
                printf("cannot open file.\n");
                exit(1);
        }
        putc('A',fp);   /* write the char 'A' */
        fclose(fp);
}
```

*FILE *fopen(name,mode)*
*char *name;*
*char *mode;*

The **fopen( )** function is used to open a file for buffered I/O operations. The **name** specifies the name of the file and **mode** is a string that specifies how the file will be accessed. Here is a list of the **mode** options:

r	open file for read only
w	open file for write only
a	open file for write and append on to the end
rw	open file for read/write mode

If the file is opened using **w**, any preexisting file by the same name will be erased. To add to a file, use **a** to append to the end.

A **fopen( )** returns a file pointer of type **FILE** if successful, and a 0 if unsuccessful.

The following function will open a file for read/write mode. In this example, the name of the file is passed to the function and, if successful, the file pointer is returned.

```
FILE *op_file(name)
char *name;
{
        FILE *fp;
        if((fp=fopen(name,"rw"))==0) {
                printf("cannot open file");
        }
        return fp;
}
```

getc(fp)
FILE *fp;

The **getc( )** function returns the next character from the file pointed to by **fp**, the file pointer.

For example, the following program opens a file called **test** for input and reads a character at a time until an EOF character is found. Each character read is printed on the screen.

```
main()
{
        FILE *fp;
        char ch;
        if((fp=fopen("test","r"))==0) {
                printf("cannot open file");
                exit(1);
        }
        do {
                ch=getc(fp);
                putchar(ch);
        } while(ch!=EOF);
        fclose(fp);
}
```

getchar( )

The **getchar( )** function returns the next character from the console.

The following function will read a string of digits entered at the console and return its integer value.

```
get_num()
{
        char s[80], *temp;
        temp=s;
        do {
                *temp=getchar(); /* read a digit */
                if(isdigit(*temp)) temp++;
        } while (*(temp-1)!='\r'); /* until return */
        *temp='\0'; /* null terminate */
        return(atoi(s));
}
```

char gets(s)
*char *s;*

The **gets( )** function is used to read a string of characters from the keyboard and put the string into character array s. Input is terminated when a carriage return is typed or an EOF character is received. Neither the carriage return nor the EOF character becomes part of string s, however. The s will be null terminated after the call. The **gets( )** returns a pointer to s or a null if an error or EOF is encountered.

Generally, **gets( )** allows the use of backspace and tabs. Some implementations may allow other special editing characters as well.

This program example will input a string from the keyboard and print it out backward on the screen:

```
main()
{
        char s[80];
        register int t;
        printf("enter a string: ");
        gets(s);
        for(t=strlen(s);t;--t) putchar(s[t]);
}
```

*char *malloc(size)*
unsigned size;

Called **alloc( )** on some systems, **malloc( )** is used to allocate a certain number, **size**, of characters of free memory and return a pointer to the beginning of it. The **malloc( )** function is part of the dynamic allocation routines.

If an allocation request fails—that is, if there is insufficient memory to fill the request—a null pointer is returned.

You always must be very careful to make sure that you receive a valid pointer from **malloc( )**.

This is the general form of a program that will allocate 80 bytes of memory and then free them.

```
main( )
{
    char *p;
    p=malloc(80);
    if(!p) {
        printf("out of memory \n");
        exit(2);
    }
    .
    .
    .
    free(p);
}
```

open(name,mode)
*char *name*
int mode;

The **open( )** function is used to open a file for unbuffered I/O. It returns an integer file descriptor on success and a −1 on failure.

The **name** is any valid file name and **mode** determines the method of access. This shows the values **mode** may have:

> 0 read only
> 1 write only
> 2 read/write

Keep in mind that **open( )** will fail if the specified file does not exist; **open( )** cannot be used to create a file.

The following function will open a file for unbuffered write-only access if it exists; if it does not exist, it will be created:

```
op_file(name)
{
        int fd;
        if((fd=open(name,2))==-1)
                if((fd=creat(name,0))==-1)
                        printf("cannot open file\n");
        return fd;
}
```

printf(control, arglist)
*char *fmt;*

The **printf( )** function is the generalized console output function. It can be used to display any of the C built-in data types as well as strings. It also permits the use of field specifiers to control the way that the information looks on the screen. (See Chapter 6, which gives a complete explanation of **printf( )**.)

After the following statements are executed

```
count=10;
printf("count is: %d",count);
```

the screen of your computer will display

```
count is: 10
```

putc(ch, fp)
char ch;
*FILE *fp;*

The **putc( )** function is used to write a character to a file previously opened using the buffered I/O function **fopen( )**, which returns **fp**. It will return **ch** after each successful write and an **EOF** character upon reaching an end-of-file.

The following function can be used to write a string to the specified file:

```
wr_string(s,fp)
char *s;
FILE *fp;
{
        while(*s) if(putc(*s++,fp)==EOF) {
                        printf("end-of-file");
                        return;
                }
}
```

read(fd,buffer,bufsize)
int fd;
int bufsize;
char *buffer;

The **read( )** is the unbuffered file I/O system's read function. It will read a number, **bufsize**, of characters into the region of memory pointed to by **buffer**. The **fd** must have been returned by a successful call to **open( )**.

If **read( )** is successful, it will return the number of bytes read. If an end-of-file is reached with no bytes having been read, the function will return 0. The **read( )** will return −1 on error.

The following function will read a buffer full of data from the specified file:

```
rd_buf(buf,fd,size)
char *buf;
int fd;
int size;
{
        if(read(fd,buf,size)==-1) {
                printf("error in read");
                return(-1);
        }
}
```

scanf(control,arglist)
*char *control;*

A **scanf( )** is a generalized input function that will read information from the console and place it, properly formatted, into the variables in **arglist**. Each argument in **arglist** must be a pointer.

A complete description of **scanf( )** is found in Chapter 6.

The following program will read a string and an integer from the keyboard:

```
main()
{
        int x;
        char s[80];
        printf("enter a string and an integer:");
        scanf("%s%d",s,&x);
}
```

*char *strcat(s1,s2)*
*char *s1,*s2;*

The **strcat( )** function appends string s2 to the end of **s1**. Both strings must have been null-terminated and the result is null-terminated. A **strcat( )** returns a pointer to **s1**.

The following code fragment will print **hello there** on the screen:

```
char first[20],second[10];
strcpy(first,"hello");
strcpy(second," there");
strcat(s1,s2);
printf(s1);
```

*char *strcmp(s1,s2)*
*char *s1, *s2*

The **strcmp( )** function compares two null-terminated strings and returns 0 if they are equal. If **s1** is lexicographically greater than **s2**, a positive number is returned; otherwise, a negative number is returned. (Some implementations may return the first character that does not match instead, so check your C compiler manual.)

For example, the following function can be used as a password verification routine:

```
password()
{
        char s[80],*strcmp();
        printf("enter password: ");
        gets(s);
        if(strcmp(s,"pass")) {
                printf("invalid password\n");
                return 0;
        }
        return 1;
}
```

*char *strcpy(s1,s2)*
*char *s1, *s2;*

A **strcpy( )** is used to copy the contents of **s2** into **s1**. The **s2** must be a pointer to a null-terminated string. The **strcpy( )** function returns a pointer to **s1**.

The following code fragment will copy **hello** into string **str**:

```
char *str;
if(str=malloc(80)) {
        printf("out of memory");
        exit(1);
}
strcpy(str,"hello");
```

strlen(s)
*char *s;*

The **strlen( )** function returns the length of the null-terminated string pointed to by s.

The following example will print the number **5** on the screen.

```
strcpy(s,"hello");
printf("%d",strlen(s));
```

tolower(ch);
char ch;

A **tolower( )** returns the lowercase equivalent of **ch** if **ch** is a letter; other-wise, **ch** is returned unchanged.

For example,

```
putchar(tolower('Q'));
```

displays **q**, while

```
putchar(tolower('!'));
```

displays !.

toupper(ch)
char ch;

A **toupper( )** returns the uppercase equivalent of **ch** if **ch** is a letter; otherwise, **ch** is returned unchanged.

For example,

```
putchar(toupper('a'));
```

displays **A**, while

```
putchar(toupper('!'));
```

displays !.

write(fd,buffer,bufsize)
int fd, bufsize;
*char *buffer;*

The **write( )** function is used to write a number of characters called **bufsize** from **buffer** to the file specified in **fd**. It is part of the unbuffered I/O system. The **fd** must have been returned by a successful call to **open( )** or **creat( )**.

On success, **write( )** returns the number of characters written; otherwise −1 is returned.

The following function will write a buffer of data to the file specified:

```
wr_buf(buf,fd,size)
char *buf;
int fd;
int size;
{
        if(write(fd,buf,size)==-1) {
                printf("error in write");
                return -1;
        }
        return 0;
}
```

INDEX